Product Design Styling

Product Design Styling

Peter Dabbs

Laurence King Publishing

LAURENCE KING

Published by Laurence King Publishing
361–373 City Road
London EC1V 1LR
United Kingdom
Tel: +44 20 7841 6900
Email: enquiries@laurenceking.com
www.laurenceking.com

A catalogue record for this book is available from the
British Library

ISBN: 978-1-78627-784-8

Design: Blok Graphic, London
Picture research: Giulia Hetherington

Printed in China

Laurence King Publishing is committed to ethical and
sustainable production. We are proud participants in
The Book Chain Project®.
bookchainproject.com

**BOOK
CHAIN
PROJECT**

Dedicated to Tim Ball whose passion and
drive for product design inspired us all

Contents

Introduction

Learning objectives

- Question how appearance affects how products are perceived (page 11).

- Explain the importance of a reliable styling process (page 12).

- Outline ideation techniques such as MAYA and Osborn's Checklist (page 12).

Introduction

Product styling is the considered act of giving form to an idea, 'a skill used by designers to add value to products without changing their technical performance', as Mike Baxter puts it in his textbook *Product Design* (1995). Styling perception must be developed if the designer is successfully and efficiently to design products that will strike a chord with the target customer. Some designers are blessed with natural styling instincts, but those without this gift can learn it. This book breaks down the styling process into its main constituents, with explanations and illustrations to inform designers of all levels.

In the early stages of concept design, product designers are expected to produce a range of solutions from a design brief, considering many different requirements along the way. At this stage it is common to focus on functional innovation and styling, since those are what will sell the concepts to the client. As the product is developed, the original form may need to be adjusted to satisfy certain requirements more successfully. Consumer products are a compromise of many elements, including function, ergonomics, environment, manufacturing, cost, serviceability and aesthetics. But any one of these can become a focal point, thereby

Product styling is the considered act of giving form to an idea.

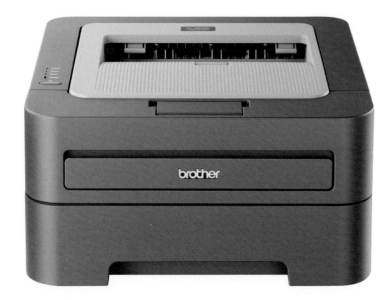

A Designed to blend into its environment: Brother HL-2240D printer

B Purely functional: adjustable spanner

C Functional design: Anglepoise
Type 75 Mini lamp

influencing the final appearance, and considered styling perception is
crucial if you as a designer are to select the most suitable visual options.

Some concepts will not require additional visual elaboration, because
their functional form may be characterful and distinctive enough
already. The customer may even prefer a design that is visually 'quiet'
and blends into its environment, as illustrated by **fig. A**. An adjustable
spanner, for example, is a distinctive and interesting-looking product,
yet it has not been styled (**fig. B**). Its form is purely functional and cost-
effective. So if a product looks favourable against the competition with a
functional form (**fig. C**), it may be a good idea to leave it that way.

The goal of product styling is not always to create beauty. A more
visually robust, playful, quiet or brand-focused style may be appropriate
in some contexts. Regardless of the chosen theme, the design should
always appear harmonious. You must learn to spot and improve
unappealing details, or risk creating products that consumers perceive
as undesirable or low-quality.

By targeting the customer's aspirations and creating several styling
options for review, you can reduce the subjectivity of product styling,
and 'move logically towards an "ideal" design' that will appeal to the
majority of the chosen market (see Del Coates, *Watches Tell More
Than Time*, 2003). The challenge for the designer arises when styling
functionally innovative products that may have odd proportions, but the

arsenal of styling techniques, knowledge and references in this book will enable you to achieve good results with even the most demanding of design briefs.

We have included several examples of car design in this book. This is because of the commercial importance of the automobile's appearance, and to expand into more complex styling methods than are commonly found in product design. Automotive designers have been developing complex styling techniques for decades, and some can be effectively applied to other categories. Once you understand these methods and have a reliable styling process, you will be able to explore complex solutions more quickly.

It is important for designers to develop their own styling process and preferences if they are to stand out and drive future styling innovation. The classic Lamborghini Countach is anything but dull, but if every product resembled it they would all appear generic. It is often the perceived originality of a product that makes it appealing, and that is why styling innovation is so important. Products that resemble the competition can be successful, but will struggle to stand out, risk design infringement prosecution and not fulfil their potential. For a brand to be distinctive it must lead with its design and styling, not follow.

Sketching allows designers to suggest several solutions quickly, as well as being an invaluable visual tool for exploring and communicating design proposals. Many books are available to help you improve your technique in this area, but dedicated practice is key. Without a basic level of sketching it will be difficult to evolve a product's design and styling, but not impossible. Some celebrated designers produce very rough-looking sketches, while others rely on handmade prototypes, CAD (computer-aided design) or the Adobe suite (Photoshop and Illustrator).

This is not a book about how to sketch. Instead, it breaks down a structured professional styling process into digestible stages, guiding you through styling your own consumer-focused products successfully. It is aimed at helping design students and professionals (as well as engineers, teachers, marketers and entrepreneurs) improve their understanding of the subject, and enabling them to style their own products. Each stage will examine and illustrate what designers should be focusing on, how to evaluate what has been designed, and how to optimize it if required. You will become better versed in critiquing the styling of competing products, as well as your own work, and can use this awareness to produce superior designs confidently and quickly.

How to use this book

As you read, have a sketch pad and pen to hand to gain a practical understanding of each stage. Be aware that not every styling stage will relate to all categories of product. Some personal judgement and experimentation will be necessary to select the most suitable styling stages for a particular product. For new products, it is preferable to begin styling once the functional elements have been defined. This allows you to establish the constraints you have to work with, as well as the areas where creative freedom can be expressed. From a design perspective, it is good practice to consider styling early in every project, so that the proportions can be optimized. If styling without constraints, be aware that the design will almost certainly need modification as it continues its journey towards production. Try to expand on the contents of this book by challenging and innovating as much as possible, since innovative ideas can generate unique styling trends that will make the future of product design more exciting. It is likely that you will not agree with all the information in this book, so embrace your opinions and record them for testing on future designs; they will help you to develop a more distinctive style.

Start looking

Before starting the styling process, it is important to realize that product designers are visual people, who use their eyes to examine and question all kinds of objects that they encounter every day. If you are new to the subject, get into the habit of observing, questioning and visually dissecting products when out and about or around the home. Question everything: Why is that attractive? What makes something else unpleasant? How could it be improved? What does the appearance say about the product? Seek out exciting new products, or classic, iconic products. Examine them in real life to understand their form better and work out what makes them special. This is how you will develop your 'styling eye', which will enable you to detect and remedy flaws in your own designs. Look at **fig. D**. The styling of the razor at the top appears more modern owing to the use of contemporary themes that were not typically associated with this product category before 2007. The tapered silhouette, aerodynamic handle, textured grip, flowing lines and shiny digital display all make it stand out against the more dated design below it, and the functionally innovative cutting head, designed to allow maximum movement, naturally provides a new appearance.

Introduction

D Philips Norelco Arcitec Electric Razor, 2007, and Philips Philishave HQ4411/88, 2001

The styling process

The concept generation stage is when designers are expected to produce several concepts that demonstrate functional innovation and visual prowess, and which could ultimately be manufactured. Designing concepts requires an awareness of the target customer and the competition, as well as a disciplined visual awareness. Having a reliable styling process will help you to create more visually appealing concepts in less time. Once a visual direction is chosen, you will feel confident in justifying the aesthetic reasoning behind your decisions, and suggest viable solutions when functional modifications are required. The following styling stages expand on the most important areas of product design styling. It is advisable to experiment by sketching to understand and absorb the information fully. Visual examples of each stage can be found at the end of each chapter, and in series at the end of the book for greater clarity.

Styling innovation

Styling is all about experimentation, since there is more than one way to style any product. Use the following information as a guide to develop and inform your own unique styling process.

Styling innovation is what excites customers visually and helps manufacturers to stay ahead of the competition, but it is common to feel at a loss for design ideas. The list on the following page is based on 'Osborn's Checklist' and can spark design and styling inspiration. The original list was compiled by Alex F. Osborn, an advertising executive who developed brainstorming as a creative tool in 1953. Go through it and use the suggestions as inspiration to create various styling options.

You can also try changing or omitting one or more of the styling stages described in this book to create a different aesthetic. Stretch your imagination and try to be unpredictable.

MAYA

The term MAYA, which stands for 'Most Advanced Yet Acceptable', was created by the industrial designer Raymond Loewy in the 1940s and is still relevant today. It suggests that designers should innovate as much as possible during the concept stage, regardless of the type of product

Osborn's Checklist:

Substitute
Try another approach, position, shape, surface or material. Can you combine the elements, shapes, purposes or ideas?

Adapt
Change the silhouette, proportions, shapes, lines or surfaces. How else could it be used? What else is like this?

Modify
Alter the proportions, colours, meaning, motion or shape. Can you give it a new angle?

Magnify
Can it be duplicated, multiplied or exaggerated? Can anything be added? Height, length, strength?

Eliminate
What can be removed? Made smaller, lighter, lower or split?

Rearrange
Swap components, alter the pattern or layout, go backwards, upside down?

Combine
Combine ideas, purposes or appeals? A blend, alloy or ensemble?

Based on Alex F. Osborn, *L'arte della creativity: Principi e procedure di creative problem solving* (Milan: Franco Angeli, 1992)

or the preferences of the customer, then simplify the design, keeping only the most innovative features. The amount of simplification will depend on the customer's preferences. The design should also possess enough 'common form' (stereotypical form commonly associated with the product type) to bring it close to the customer's visual expectations. This creates the confidence that it will be fit for its function.

'I have always wondered quite how designer Flaminio Bertoni ... managed to clear his mind of every pre-conceived idea of what a car should look like, and design a shape like ... nothing that had ever been seen before.'

Peter Stevens, automotive designer

Chapter 1

Choosing a visual theme

Learning objectives

- Demonstrate an understanding of customer aspirations, user profiles, competition analysis and cultural trends (page 16).

- Create a mood board for a design concept (page 20).

- Discuss brand styling and how it is applied across several products (page 21).

Chapter 1
Choosing a visual theme

Customer aspirations

Before styling can begin, a decision must be made about the visual theme the product should embody. By selecting a theme that will connect with the target customer's expectations and aspirations, the subjectivity of product styling can be reduced. Our perception of an object depends on how it relates to our memories, emotions and feelings about other comparable objects. A young woman will have different tastes and values from an older man, so it's important to do some research to understand the demographic fully before putting pen to paper. Which products tend to appeal to them? What visual information do these products display? Where will the product be used or displayed? What symbolism will the buyer positively connect with? Get this right and the customer will be more likely to form an emotional bond with the product, increasing the probability of a purchase.

User profile

A user profile will provide a clear description of the target customer and help to define a visual theme to focus on. Once you have selected the target age range, say 18–35, the next step is to find out how people in that age group live their lives and what is important to them. There are several ways to gain accurate information about a target customer's desires, buying habits and aspirations. A focus group with carefully considered questions never fails to provide vital information. Where do they live? Where do they work? What is their income? What hobbies do they enjoy? Do they have children? Which websites do they visit? Record the session so that nothing is missed, and ask the group to send you a photograph of the environment where the product will be used. This way you can ensure that the design will look suitable for its environment. Magazines aimed at this age group will also contain vital visual information about products that may appeal to them, clothing they might wear and holidays they may aspire to.

This information can be analysed to create a customer persona with the values and lifestyle attributes most commonly displayed in the focus group. Surround an image of the chosen character with a series of images, taken from the internet, that describe their values, desires and aspirations. The aim is to get a feeling of what the target customer will find visually appealing, based on the objects they value.

Competitor styling analysis

Once a design brief has been provided, one of the first things designers do is scan the competition to discover the functional and visual icons. Which is more prominent, styling or function? What styling themes are there? Which products are most successful and why? Designers add character and meaning (semantics) to products through their visual symbolism and association, which in turn affect the perception of the product.

A useful way of gauging what appeals to a target customer is to use a tool known as the Semantic Differential Scale (SDS), created by the American psychologist Charles Osgood in the 1960s (**fig. 1.1**).

This scale has opposing words down the left- and right-hand sides, which should be chosen carefully by the designer to indicate how close a concept is to the target customer's ideal design. A group of target customers can be invited to view a product and plot their visual opinions in the columns between the words, adding a point closer to the word that describes their feelings most accurately.

1.1 SDS: comparing the appearance of two different designs (from J.G. Snider and C.E. Osgood, *Semantic Differential Technique: A Sourcebook*, Chicago: Aldine, 1969)

	1	2	3	4	5	6	7	8	9	10	
Simple			A					B			Complex
Smooth			A		B						Rough
Graceful		A			B						Awkward
Passive			A					B			Aggressive
Weak				A					B		Strong
Light		A						B			Heavy
Rounded				A				B			Angular
Curved			A				B				Straight
Soft			A				B				Hard
Slow					A				B		Fast
Feminine			A						B		Masculine

Design A ○
Design B ●

If the group is asked to review the appearance of a popular competitor product, the results could inform the designer about the most suitable themes to develop before styling begins. For example, the group may decide that a new design should be 'curved' and 'simple', two attributes found in the left-hand column.

The SDS can also be used to review a range of concept designs. This will guide the designer as to which direction to pursue. The group can then be invited to plot where their 'ideal' design would appear on the scale, to inform the designer which styling direction to take from the present position. For example, the group may indicate a preference for a 'lighter'-looking design, prompting the designer to find ways of creating a more compact package or less bulky styling.

Once a few design illustrations have been completed, it is also possible to check the target customer's reactions to them. The more relevant individuals that are involved with this research process, the more telling the results will be. Be aware that this should be used only as a guide, however, since the general public is not always in tune with advanced design and styling.

The zeitgeist

The zeitgeist is the cultural trends that capture our imagination at a particular period. These can be translated by designers into visual influences to make the styling of a product appear current. A classic

1.2 Left, Cadillac Coupe de Ville tail fins, 1959. Right, Apple iMac G4, 2002

1.3 Bang & Olufsen BeoLab
19 wireless subwoofer, 2013

example of zeitgeist can be seen in the styling of American cars of the 1950s and 60s, with their innovative fin designs (**fig. 1.2**). The designers added aeronautical-inspired elements to the vehicles to try and capture the power and speed of the jet aircraft that were so new and fascinating at the time. Aeronautics remains an attractive theme for some designers, but it is no longer the zeitgeist.

A user-friendly aesthetic, to encourage new technology into our homes, was the zeitgeist at the turn of the millennium. Apple embraced this with the iMac G4 (**fig. 1.2**), in which simple shapes and transparency disguised the complexity of the operating system. A strong example of the current zeitgeist is environmental friendliness and efficiency. That is why the hexagon appears in many products, influenced by nature's honeycomb. An example is the B&O BeoLab 19 speaker (**fig. 1.3**). This uses a polygon rather than a hexagon, but achieves a similar visual. As a designer, you must stay in touch with these shifting trends so that you can use them to add spice and originality to your work.

'Product personality influences our perceptions. Think about how quickly we form expectations about someone simply based on how they dress or present themselves.'

Stephen P. Anderson, experience designer

1.4 Eco-friendly mood board

Creating a mood board

Designers take visual inspiration from many sources, most commonly nature, architecture, science fiction, vehicles and other products. Once a suitable visual theme has been chosen to connect with the target customer, you can collate a handful of relevant images that convey the desired visual and emotional connections. These images can be grouped as a physical or digital collage to form a mood board. The mood board shown in **fig. 1.4**, for example, evokes an eco-friendly theme. Mood boards can be used for inspiration while styling, and become the visual specification for a product. You may decide to create additional mood boards that display the target customer's persona or lifestyle, as well as the emotions the design should evoke. The more connected you are to the target customer, the more successful the visual design will be.

You can now dissect specific elements from the mood board and use them as inspiration while styling, experimenting with the shapes, forms and textures found in the imagery until you achieve a satisfactory and relevant design language for the product. Examine the silhouettes, lines, shapes and surfaces in the mood board and identify the elements that make the most powerful visual statement (honeycomb hexagons, for example). This increases the likelihood that the customer will subconsciously notice the visual associations. Most people can

recognize a flower's silhouette, so if the language of the product's form reflects this shape, the customer will probably associate it with nature and eco-friendliness. If the chosen shapes become too obscure, the meaning you are trying to portray will be lost. The elements you choose should not always be exact replicas of those found in the mood board, but should be abstracted for subtlety. The aim is to inject one or more styling elements into the product to suggest the relevant meaning to the observer. There is no right or wrong result, since every designer's vision will be slightly different. What does matter is that the chosen form language has a connection to the original theme, and moves you. If it does, it will probably move the customer as well.

By creating several styling options, you increase your chance of a successful outcome. No matter how good a first sketch may appear, always aim to create various styling options using different elements from the mood board. Look at **fig. 1.5**, which has an eco-friendly vibe, and think about where the inspiration may have come from.

1.5 Design details of Renault Twizy ZE concept car, 2009

Brand styling

When challenged with a brief to style a product for a particular brand, you must study the company in order to embody it visually with a unique

1.6 Part of the Dyson product range, including Dyson DC24 Ball Upright, 2019

and meaningful form language. Once you understand the brand's vision, culture, personality and unique characteristics, assemble a brand-focused mood board to help you develop your styling ideas. These ideas will form a brand-focused design language that can be used to bond a range of products visually as a family, while also distinguishing them from the competition.

These visual links – brand DNA – are often in the form of matching silhouettes, lines, shapes, surfaces, materials or colours. The aim is to make this visual DNA distinctive enough to stand out from the competition, creating brand recognition and loyalty. The range of products seen in **fig. 1.6** blends functional design and simple geometry for an efficient yet friendly appearance.

'Between two products equal in price, function and quality, the better-looking will outsell the other.'

Raymond Loewy, product designer

Chapter overview

Understand the demographic and create a fictitious user persona with the following insights:

01 | Which products tend to appeal to these consumers?

02 | What visual information do these products display?
Where will the product be used or displayed?

03 | What symbolism will these consumers connect with positively?
Where do they live?

04 | Where do they work? What is their income?

05 | What hobbies do they enjoy? Do they have children?

06 | Which websites do they visit?

07 | Select a visual theme that will connect with the target customer's expectations and aspirations.

08 | Consider using the Semantic Differential Scale to assess the target customer's favourite products, and ensure the theme has these qualities.

09 | Assess the zeitgeist, the cultural trends that capture our imagination at a particular period. Use these visual references to make product styling appear more current.

10 | Create a mood board for relevant inspiration while styling.

Chapter 2

Silhouette

Learning objectives

- Define the term 'silhouette' in relation to a product (page 26).

- Outline the steps required to develop a silhouette (page 27).

- Demonstrate how to create and use a design guide (page 28).

- Explain how internal components influence a product's outer silhouette (page 29).

- Discuss the usefulness of a functional silhouette as a starting point (page 31).

- Explain how symbolism can be incorporated into a product's silhouette (page 32).

- Outline the appropriate applications of symmetry and asymmetry (page 34).

- Discuss the importance of retaining commonly recognized features as a communication tool (page 36).

- Summarize the main points of silhouette design (page 37).

Chapter 2
Silhouette

A two-dimensional (2D) silhouette is the best place to start the
styling process, since it defines the boundaries of the product. It is
the outermost shape that often packages mechanical or electrical
components, or occupants (human, animal or parts thereof). The
silhouette is one of the first things we notice when we look at a
product, and it can provide a great deal of visual information, including
function and personality. A silhouette can also present ergonomic
visual information (how users should interact with the product), to
improve first-time use. As can be seen in **fig. 2.1**, an invitingly shaped,
hand-sized protrusion will always suggest a good place to grasp or
hold a product.

Products have a better chance of standing out beside the competition
if they can be recognized by their silhouette alone. Many products
have developed distinctive silhouettes because of the particular
functions they serve, or the regulations they must adhere to. Modern
upright vacuum cleaners, for instance, have long, slim silhouettes that

2.1 Philips GC7635/30
PerfectCare Pure Steam
Generator iron, 2013

reduce the user's need to bend, while minimizing weight for carrying and size for storage. Supercars tend to have a low, wedge-like silhouette when viewed in side profile, making them stand out instantly beside more common vehicles, even from a distance.

Developing a silhouette

The following chapters focus on how to develop the exterior styling of a product. Sketching a rough silhouette is an important first step, because it defines the product boundaries and enables you to judge better where to position the external features (a digital display, user controls, wheels and so on). The lamp in **fig. 2.2** has an instantly recognizable silhouette that makes it stand out. Its smooth design is also tactile; running a finger along its surface turns LEDs on or off.

You should create a new silhouette around a scaled package drawing or design guide (see page 28). A package drawing illustrates the scaled dimensions and positions of the internal components or occupants, allowing the designer to explore different design options and ergonomics. Using a package drawing is accurate but time-consuming, and allows you to experiment by repositioning or replacing internal components. **Fig. 2.3** is an example of a package drawing, with the

2.2 Fonckel One Luminaire lamp, 2012, designed by Philip Ross

2.3 Dyson Supersonic hairdryer patent, 2017, silhouette highlighted (modified image)

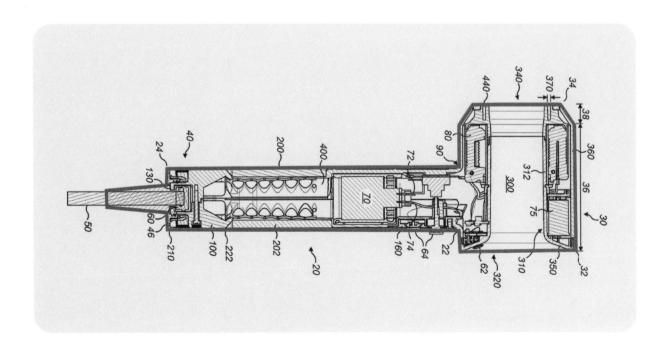

silhouette highlighted in pink. If the designer wanted to move the motor (#70) found in the centre of the handle, for example, it could be traced and repositioned. If this were a product designed to house occupants, these would also have to be illustrated to ensure they could be included.

Creating a design guide

A design guide is a 2D image of an existing product that is used as an underlay for you to sketch over, helping you to create several viable concepts quickly. It is a quick alternative to a package drawing, and is better suited to products that require only a styling update and no internal component modifications. When using a design guide, you must still understand why certain areas of the existing silhouette look the way they do, since the new design may require similar features. For example, the iron seen in **fig. 2.4** needs a flat soleplate at the base, and the heel rest at the rear allows it to be seated vertically. The new silhouette must also contain these two flat features, unless the designer can innovate with new and improved solutions. A new silhouette that doesn't pass inside the design guide lines (right-hand image) should be viable, since the internal components can still be packaged.

To create a design guide, first evaluate which viewing angle suits the particular product best. If no modifications are to be made to the internal components, choose a 2D view to match the way the product will be seen or used most of the time. You can increase your chances of grabbing a customer's attention by focusing on the most visually important view first. With a digital radio, for example, that would be the front view, whereas a top view would make sense for a wristwatch.

2.4 Philips Affinia GC160/07 dry iron. Right: Design guide

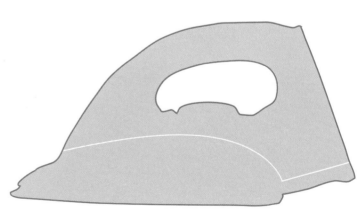

Print out the 2D image at a manageable scale, place a sheet of layout paper over it, and trace its silhouette and main visual features using a thick, dark pen. This traced silhouette can now be used as an underlay to help develop feasible new silhouettes. Design guides increase efficiency and minimize the risk of disappointing the client, who will naturally expect the final product to resemble the original sketches that they will review.

Styling without design guides can encourage creativity, but if they are ignored the sketches will have flaws that will need correcting as the design is developed, potentially destroying the feel of the original drawing. Concept cars, with their typically impractical low roofs and other extreme proportions, can look great on paper but are an example of what can happen when design guides are not used.

Silhouette and internal components

Before a new silhouette can be created, you must know the rough position and size of the internal components. A design guide will not tell you where the internal components or occupants are, but it may provide a clue. The dog lead seen in **fig. 2.5** has a soft, playful silhouette for functional, ergonomic and stylistic reasons. The left-hand part of the silhouette houses a large ratchet wheel around which the lead wraps, and which stops it from extending when the top button is pressed. A circle is the perfect shape for this half of the silhouette, because it mirrors the main internal component. The right-hand part of the silhouette is elliptical,

2.5 Flexi New Comfort retractable dog lead, 2013

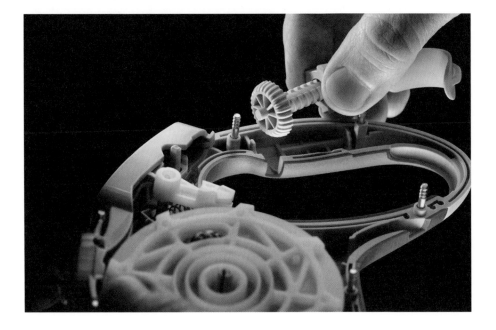

2.6 As above, showing the packaged components that influence the silhouette

forming a neat handle that is ergonomic and complements the circular side. The button above it depresses into the case, so internal space is needed to house its mechanism.

The dog lead has been tightly packaged, leaving little space to move areas of the silhouette closer to the internal components (**fig. 2.6**). If the brief were to restyle this product, there would be three options: 1. Adjust the silhouette outwards, making the product slightly larger, to provide more options for silhouette design; 2. Reduce the size of internal components if possible, to bring areas of the silhouette inwards; or 3. Leave the silhouette as it is and update other aspects of the design.

Once you understand which areas of the design guide's silhouette can be modified, you can start work on designing the new silhouette. Sketch a straight line that will be the ground plane for the product to rest on (if it makes sense to do so), and use the design guide to lightly trace the main exterior features of the new design. The principal features of the games console (**fig. 2.7**), for example, are the digital display, the

2.7 Sony PlayStation Vita games console, 2012. Below, with silhouette and main visual features highlighted

controls and the speaker holes; for a vehicle, on the other hand, they would be the wheels, the lights and the cabin windows. Don't worry about the styling of these features at this stage, because the primary concern is to do with their position and scale, to see how they affect the product's overall appearance.

Functional silhouettes

When designing a new type of product, it is advisable to sketch a purely functional silhouette first, since that may already be distinctive enough. A functional silhouette disregards style and simply wraps the product in a utilitarian and ergonomic manner. This could be as simple as sketching rectangles around rectangular internal components, assuming those shapes are in line with the target customer's preferences (see page 20). Some products must have functional silhouettes that echo the packaged components or occupants closely, to make them as compact as possible; a mobile phone or a running shoe come to mind. Other products may be given more distance from the internal components to improve ergonomics, stability, safety or styling (a television remote control or an electric guitar, for example).

If a functional silhouette is undesirable or unsuitable for the target customer, you can begin to modify areas that do not disrupt the function or ergonomics by injecting originality. While sketching, many designers experiment by 'ghosting' faint lines until they find the most desirable option. Don't be too precious about the silhouette's styling at this stage, since it may need refining later on. Once a decision is made, the chosen lines can be darkened with a thicker pen or by applying more force on the page. Ensure that important functional design details, such as buttons or handles, are scaled correctly for the intended customers.

Silhouette lines that do not need to be functionally straight can be given some curvature if you wish to reduce the visual rigidity of the design. Sketch lines with curvature by pivoting from the wrist or elbow, so that

---

'I always start off with a silhouette. The silhouette says something. It says noble, it says playful, it says gorgeous, it says efficient, it says opulent.'

Freeman Thomas, automotive designer

your arm creates a natural arc for the pen. Some silhouettes must have straight lines because of their function or environment; microwave ovens and washing machines always have straight sides to keep them compact and allow them to fit neatly into kitchens. Sleek-looking profiles tend to be easier on the eye, so if possible keep the silhouette's transitions to a minimum, or as smooth as possible across the packaged components, unless a more angular style is desired.

Also keep in mind that not all mechanical components should be hidden away, and some can add to the visual appeal, depending on the target market. Motorbike designers excite the customer by displaying all or part of the engine, as if to offer a glimpse of the power hidden beneath. Watch designers sometimes expose the movement, offering a fascinating glimpse of the beauty of engineering.

Symbolic silhouettes

Another option open to you as a designer is the symbolic silhouette, which uses a relevant symbolic shape to add character. A product that doesn't have many external constraints, such as an external hard drive, may not have a functionally distinctive or visually appealing silhouette. In this case you may decide to choose a symbolic yet functional shape

2.8 The Alessi S.p.A. Diva watering can, 2011, uses a symbolic silhouette design

that is linked to the original theme and mood board. Symbolic shapes should be abstracted to simplify their form, and manipulated to fit the design guide or package drawing. The aim is to give the viewer a taste of the chosen shape; it should not be too obvious where it was derived from. This way the viewer will connect subconsciously with the semantics of the shape, but not dwell on them. Simple geometry such as circles or ellipses can be used to create timeless silhouettes if they can work with the function of the product. Refer to the mood board (see page 20) to get inspiration for a symbolic silhouette, and consider how it may need to be modified to improve usability. By changing the silhouette of a watering can to something more animated, it is possible to create a product that stands out among the competition and puts a smile on the customer's face. Another way to analyse a product's silhouette visually is to darken the entire exterior shape to emphasize the main outline, as seen in **fig. 2.8**.

Fig. 2.9 shows two examples of how to take a relevant image, abstract its symbolic silhouette and incorporate it into a product.

2.9 Silhouettes providing inspiration for product design

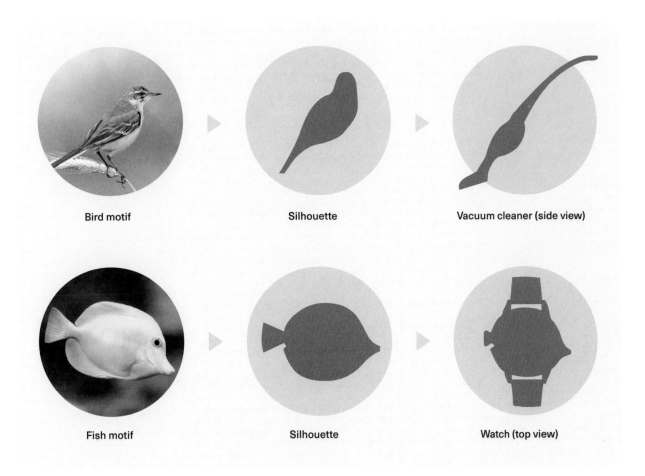

Bird motif   Silhouette   Vacuum cleaner (side view)

Fish motif   Silhouette   Watch (top view)

Symmetrical versus asymmetrical

A silhouette can be symmetrical, and therefore visually balanced, or asymmetrical and visually unbalanced. Washing machines and many other white goods tend to have symmetrical silhouettes with functional advantages, such as making them easy to install in compact home environments. The radio seen in **fig. 2.10** has a symbolic silhouette that is symmetrical when viewed from the front or side, providing a soft-looking, touch-friendly surface that encourages the user to interact with it. The features (buttons and speakers) are mirrored across the front of the product, and the digital display commands the centre.

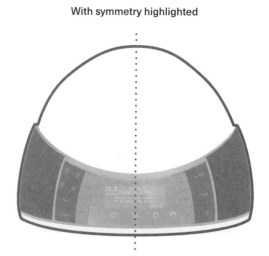

With symmetry highlighted

2.10 Pure Twilight radio, 2012, with symmetrical silhouette

Note that the radio's speakers (pink) and button clusters (green) echo the curvature of the silhouette, creating visual harmony. The centre height of the main black volume is a third of the total height of the product, which maximizes the volume of the lamp while also being proportionally appealing (see Chapter 3).

Vehicles are dynamic products, so asymmetrical side-profile silhouettes are common because they add visual impact. The silhouette in **fig. 2.11** has been designed with the highlighted cabin window volume biased to the rear of the vehicle, providing an unbalanced and therefore more dynamic silhouette.

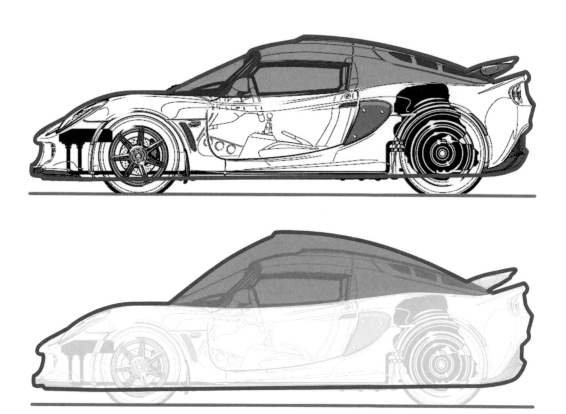

If more headroom were required in this example to improve entry to the vehicle, the silhouette could be adjusted as in the second image. But note that this taller silhouette is less elegant, less aerodynamic and less appealing proportionally than the original.

Let's take the electric guitar as another example. **Fig. 2.12** is a classic example of a distinctive, attractive, yet functional silhouette that is instantly recognizable. The neck of a guitar is purely functional, so this part of its silhouette will be identical to that of other guitars, unless you can invent an innovative alternative. The head stock and main body,

2.11 Lotus Exige, 2006, with silhouette in purple (modified image). Below, with silhouette altered to accommodate extra height

2.12 Fender Stratocaster, 1954–present

however, can be pretty much any shape, as long as it is comfortable enough to play and provides enough space for the strings, bridge, controls, pickups and electronics. The curves in the sides of the silhouette let the guitar rest on the thigh when played sitting down, and allow the guitarist's chest to rest more comfortably against it. The horn shapes at the top of the main body are partly the result of ergonomic development, because they allow the guitarist's hand to reach the high notes more comfortably. You can let your imagination run wild with the rest of the silhouette, within the boundaries of the chosen theme, which is based on the target customer's preferences and aspirations.

As a designer, you should always aim to improve the functionality of a product, because that can add visual distinction to the silhouette. If the design brief is to restyle an existing product without any technical modifications, a new silhouette can make a huge difference to the final appearance.

Silhouette semantics

Product semantics refers to the visual information an object communicates to the viewer, such as what category it fits into and how it should be operated. The silhouette and visual features tend to provide most of this, so designing a unique silhouette risks making it more difficult for the customer to understand, and possibly less appealing if its use is not apparent. If this is the case, the areas of interaction may need to be emphasized. A product's form will ideally communicate its function and how it can be interacted with, or at least provide confidence that the form is fit for function. The main visual elements of a stereotypical camera, for instance, are a rectangular main volume with a cylindrical lens attached to the front face (**fig. 2.13**). This is how consumers have recognized this product's category, function and ergonomics for decades.

Dispose of the cylindrical lens and the semantics is reduced. The absence of common form may diminish some customers' confidence in a product, and may even put them off. Others, of course, may be attracted to the exciting new form, which is why it's important to know whom you are designing for. You should always try to style intelligent silhouettes that are fit for function and have enough common form for customers to understand. This should be balanced with a silhouette that is distinctive enough to stand out among the competition.

2.13 Canon PowerShot G9 X
Mark II digital camera, 2016

Silhouette optimization

The sketch in **fig. 2.14** was originally drawn without a grid, but the designer has intuitively positioned lines and points of the silhouette so that they relate to one another, adding visual harmony. This can be optimized by using a grid, as shown. Lightly sketch vertical and horizontal lines through the edges of the silhouette's points (pink dots) and extend them across the design (blue lines). Now fill in the gaps with evenly spaced lines until a grid is formed, and reposition any points that are misaligned. The aim is to ensure that as many edges and points line up with one another as possible, to achieve a balanced design.

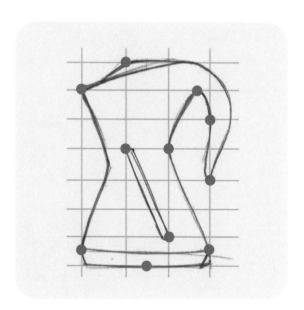

2.14 Grid used to line up visual features and silhouette points

For example, in the kettle shown on page 39, the tip of the spout is aligned horizontally with the inside arc of the handle, and the water-level indicator is parallel to the lower rear body of the silhouette, all of which creates a more harmonious appearance. With practice you will be able to do this instinctively, without having to add a grid. Remember, if a product doesn't look quite right it is usually because of proportional imperfections, so take the time to get this stage right.

Chapter overview

Choose the most appropriate 2D view to begin your silhouette design. Have your design guide ready, place a sheet of layout paper over the top and sketch a ground plane. Add any visual features that will grace the exterior, but before designing the silhouette think about the following:

01 | **Where are the internal components?**

02 | **What is the chosen theme or form language?**

03 | **Could a relevant symbolic silhouette provide more distinction?**

04 | **Will a symmetrical or asymmetrical silhouette be more suitable?**

05 | **Is there adequate common form to communicate function and interaction?**

06 | **Begin sketching the silhouette by 'ghosting' faint lines and trying not to stray too far from the design guide. Once a decision is made, the chosen silhouette lines can be darkened to make it stand out. If the final silhouette still looks generic at this stage, because of functional restrictions, more focus will be required in later stages. The silhouette will probably need minor refinement throughout the styling process. A grid is useful when optimizing the silhouette.**

Case study: Electric Kettle

Here is an example of a new silhouette design.

On the right is a sketch of an existing kettle that a client requires to be restyled into something more hi-tech and distinctive. The designer begins by understanding the design constraints and deciding which areas of the original silhouette could be modified. The spout, handle position and height must match the original product (see the faint outline on the image below right), but the rest can be manipulated to a certain extent.

This silhouette design will evolve throughout the styling process.

Original design

The new, more distinctive silhouette has already radically changed the appearance of the original, but enough common form remains in the spout and handle for it to be recognizable as a kettle.

Revised design

Chapter 3

Proportion

Learning objectives

- Define proportion in relation to a product (page 42).

- Discuss the way in which trends affect the choice of proportion (page 42).

- Explain the steps required to improve proportions (page 45).

- Demonstrate how to improve appearance through proportional adjustments (page 48).

- Apply the concepts of the Golden Ratio and organic proportional alignment to an existing product (pages 49 and 50).

- Explain how playing with proportion can draw attention to a particular feature (page 51).

- Analyse the proportions of a series of products (page 52).

- Summarize the main points of proportion design (page 56).

Chapter 3
Proportion

Once a silhouette and visual features have been roughly sketched, the next step is to evaluate their proportions. Proportion is the relationship between the overall length and height of a 2D silhouette, and how the visual features work with it and with one another. Even the slightest proportional change can affect the appearance of a design. By changing the scale or position of a feature (the diameter of a watch's chronograph dial, for instance), it is possible to alter the entire visual coherence of a product. A designer can create the most exquisite form, but if it is injected into a poorly proportioned package it will not look right. If the proportions of the humble vegetable peeler in **fig. 3.1** were squashed, for example, it would not be so elegant.

> '**Proportions ...
> separate a donkey
> from a racehorse.**'
>
> **Freeman Thomas,
> automotive designer**

3.1 Savora Swivel Blade peeler, 2013. Below, with shortened proportions, reducing its elegance

Trends

Preferred proportions change with the times. Many American cars of the 1950s and 60s were very long with vast rear overhangs (**fig. 3.3**), but nowadays more compact proportions are desirable (**fig. 3.4**). Mobile phones were large and heavy in the 1980s, and were often carried around in a shoulder bag. As batteries became more compact, so did the phones' overall size. And, of course, once the

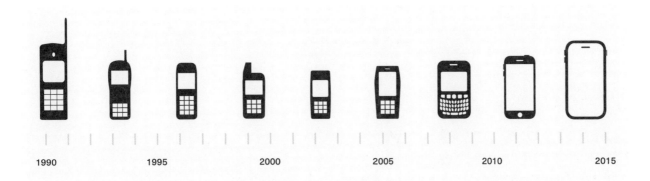

mobile phone turned into a touch-screen computer, once again the proportions were altered to make it easier to use (**fig. 3.2**).

By being aware of the current proportional trends in a particular category of product, you can either replicate or avoid the trend, resulting in a design that conforms to the norm or challenges it. New products with unexpected or extreme proportions never fail to catch the eye.

3.2 The evolution of the mobile phone

Chapter Three Proportion

3.3 Cadillac Eldorado Biarritz, 1959, with extreme proportions

3.4 Audi A3 e-tron, 2014, has more compact, modern-looking proportions

A product's overall proportions are primarily influenced by function, ergonomics, internal technology, environment, regulations and cost. Good proportions are especially important for products that are designed to attach to humans (rucksacks and watches, for example), since they should complement the user. Proportions will also affect practicality and usability. The first mobile phones were larger than a house brick, so users would never have dreamed of slipping them into a pocket as we now do daily.

One proportion that always seems to impress is slenderness. It is common for technology companies to design gadgets that are smaller than the previous model, with the aim of impressing the customer. Televisions and mobile phones have gradually become more slender as technology has advanced. This helps to make new products appear more enticing than their predecessors, but it can be achieved only by repositioning or re-engineering internal components. If you feel that a new design would benefit from proportional adjustment, first study the package and try to find areas where compromises could be made. If the changes are feasible, and the engineers and management agree, it may be possible to adjust the components or their position to achieve the proposed proportions. When product styling is vital to desirability, proportions should be agreed with the engineering team as early as possible to ensure the best visual result.

Before the Motorola Razr V3 mobile phone (**fig. 3.5**) was released in 2004, all mobile phones had chunky side profiles. The design team managed to rearrange the electrical components, allowing them to achieve a slim side-profile silhouette, one of the innovative design elements that made the phone such a huge success.

3.5 Motorola Razr V3, 2004

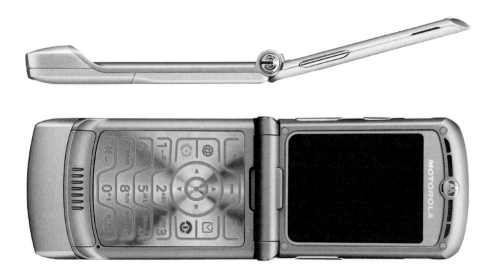

Proportional improvements

The spacing of major visual features is key to achieving good proportions, because humans instinctively look for patterns in the objects we see, and our visual system is so finely tuned that we can spot the slightest imperfections. By adjusting the position, scale or spacing of a product's major features, so that they fit neatly into a silhouette, you maximize your chances of creating visually appealing proportions.

The connection between the scale and position of a major feature, and its relationship to the product silhouette, is critical to the appearance of the product. The wheels of a car have a functional diameter and position, but the most harmonious wheel diameter is one that can be duplicated to fit equally into the vehicle's silhouette.

It's common to see wheels or wheel arches that are half the height of the vehicle, but it is not a rule. The spacing between two identical visual features should be as well proportioned as possible, because they have a visual connection. The car seen in **fig. 3.6** has a perfect three-wheel spacing at its wheelbase, and the overall height is about two wheels, which balances the design. The silhouette of this particular vehicle is fairly symmetrical in side profile, which is rare in automotive design. Only the offset positioning of the cabin and the slight taper add dynamism.

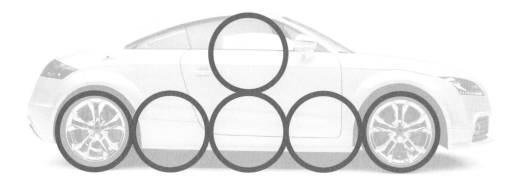

Chapter Three Proportion

3.6 Audi TT, 2000. Left, showing how wheel size and spacing defines the overall proportions

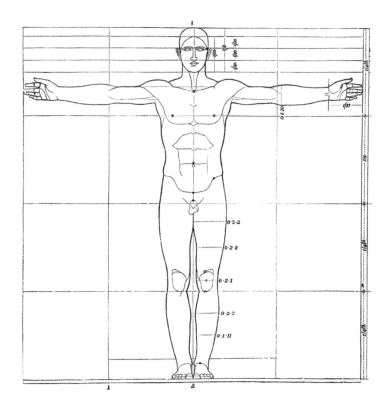

3.7 The human body divided up proportionally, after Vitruvius

If the visual features cannot be changed, the other option is to modify the silhouette for a better fit. The first-century BC architect Vitruvius and his followers maintained that the parts and whole of the human body correspond proportionally, and this could be why we often prefer well-proportioned objects. For example, **fig. 3.7** shows a man whose height matches his arm span. With his arms at his sides, his overall width is two heads. His head is about eight times smaller than the total height of his body, and so on.

It is not always safe to assume that the proportions of a competing product can be simply transferred to a new design, since they may need optimizing to work with the new silhouette and visual features.

To improve the proportions of a product, your first step is to analyse and determine its *current* proportions, and that is why it is important to have a silhouette and visual features roughly sketched out. By drawing a box around the 2D silhouette it is easier to determine its overall proportions and make adjustments if necessary. Depending on the product, the sketched box will result in a low and wide rectangle, a tall and narrow rectangle, or something closer to a square.

Square overall proportions tend to appear static, but also solid, and they suit symmetrical designs. Rectangular overall proportions are dynamic, and can emphasize a sense of motion (**fig. 3.8**).

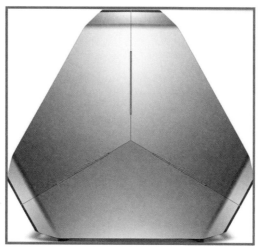

3.8 Left, Dyson Pure Cool purifying desk fan, 2016: rectangular proportions. Right, Dell Alienware Area-51 desktop computer: square proportions

It is unlikely that the overall proportions will be able to change drastically unless the product package can be adjusted, as was done with the Motorola Razr V3. A more likely scenario is that one side of the silhouette may be elongated or shortened slightly to improve the proportions. For instance, reducing the height of a product can increase its perceived width, in the same way that lengthening a silhouette can appear to reduce its width (and perceived weight), as seen in **fig. 3.9**.

Before the proportions of the silhouette can be finalized, it is essential to optimize the proportions of the visual features, since they will influence the final silhouette.

Chapter Three | Proportion

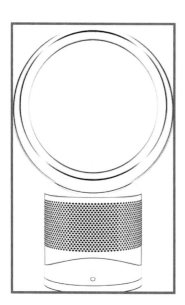

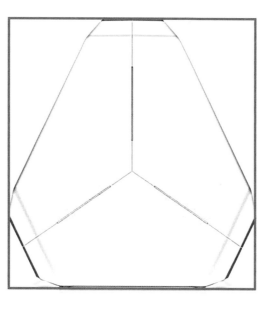

3.9 As above with height reduced, giving the illusion of a wider base (desk fan), and height increased, giving the illusion of a thinner product (computer)

Proportional design

Highlight the product's dominant visual features. Ensure that they are evenly spaced horizontally or vertically by altering their scale or position. Ideally, they will also fit evenly into the silhouette (see page 45). If they cannot be made to fit evenly because of functional restrictions, it may be possible to adjust the length or height of the silhouette to allow a better fit. Experimentation is crucial to achieving balanced proportions, which are essentially visual features positioned in a logical, orderly and related manner. If it is impossible to adjust the position of a feature, try increasing or reducing its scale instead, until it appears more evenly spaced. Take special care to ensure that the ergonomics do not suffer as a result of proportional adjustments to the visual features.

More dynamic products may require an element of 'proportional feel' from the designer that may not result in evenly spaced features. In this case, you must trust your instincts.

Fig. 3.10 shows a product that we will use to demonstrate how proportional adjustments can improve appearance. The first image is a benchmark music player design that will be used for comparison. The second image is the same design with a grid formed around the major

3.10 Music player with and without optimized proportions

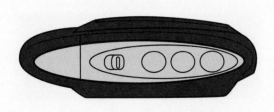

Benchmark

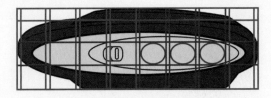

Without optimized proportions

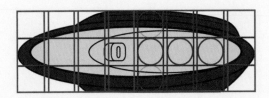

With optimized proportions

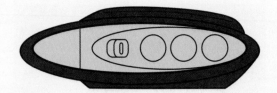

Final design

visual features (the button controls highlighted in purple). The blue grid lines were added first and the rest of the grid (pink) repeated around them. The grid tells us that the player's buttons do not fit equally into the silhouette's height, and a few other points are misaligned. The third image is the result of minor proportional changes; the height of the buttons has been increased so that they fill a third of the total height of the product (purple circles), and the intersections are aligned better with the grid. The silhouette has also been smoothed in some places. The fourth image shows the updated design. These seemingly minor alterations have cleaned up the product significantly.

Professional designers naturally experiment with proportional details by ghosting (sketching lightly) until they find a satisfactory result. For products that have few or no obvious visual features, you must instead focus on making the silhouette as balanced as possible. This can be done by tweaking the intersections of the silhouette until they link horizontally or vertically with neighbouring points or visual features. An example of this can be found at the end of this chapter. Another proportional technique that can improve visual design is the Golden Ratio.

Golden Ratio

The Golden Ratio is a classical visual theory that has been used by architects and designers for hundreds of years. When experimenting with proportions and scaling and positioning visual features, using the Golden Ratio – which is found commonly in nature – produces pleasing results. Take a square (or dimension) and extend it horizontally or vertically by 0.618 times its original length; the result is a rectangle with Golden proportions. Another way to experiment with this ratio is to take a dimension and use the additional 0.618 distance as spacing to position a neighbouring feature.

For the chair in **fig. 3.11**, the designer used the Golden Ratio to determine the size and spacing of some of the major features. The pink dimensions are 0.618 times longer than the green dimensions. This technique can be used many times in a single product, starting with the smallest features. It will take more time to experiment with, but can produce great results. If time is scarce, try spacing the visual features by a third instead, since this is close to the Golden Ratio. A product that has a bland rectangular silhouette, such as an external hard drive, may benefit from having proportions that conform to the Golden Ratio.

'Every part is disposed to unite with the whole, that it may thereby escape from its own incompleteness.'

Leonardo da Vinci, artist and inventor

3.11 Herman Miller Mirra Triflex chair, 2013 (modified image)

Organic proportional alignment

The music player in fig. 3.10 demonstrated a structured method of aligning visual features proportionally by using a grid. A more organic approach is to link design features visually. The left- and right-hand sides of the cabin window seen in **fig. 3.12** are tangential to the front and rear wheel arches, to provide visual cohesion. It is also common for components to be aligned to the central axis of circular features. The easiest way to review a design is to extend the silhouette's intersection lines inside the silhouette, and adjust the edges of any features that are close to those lines, so that they align better. This can also work the other way round, as highlighted in the second image. Take a visual feature and extend a line tangentially from it in the direction of a neighbouring feature, ensuring that they line up with each other. This may involve rotating a feature or altering its design to create a more natural visual link. Designers can detect when a product doesn't look quite right, and it is usually down to tiny proportional imperfections and misalignments.

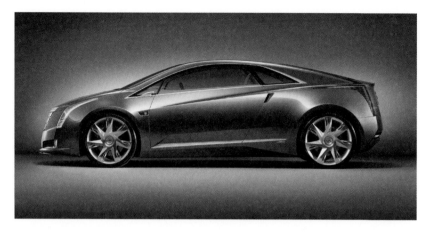

3.12 Cadillac Converj concept car, 2009. Below, highlighting lines that link to visual features

Proportional focus

The designer can highlight important features by making them appear out of proportion to the whole. The high chair in **fig. 3.13** has a proportionally large footprint for stability. This visual imbalance draws the eye to that feature, suggesting that the product is stable and safe.

3.13 Mamas & Papas Loop high chair, 2013

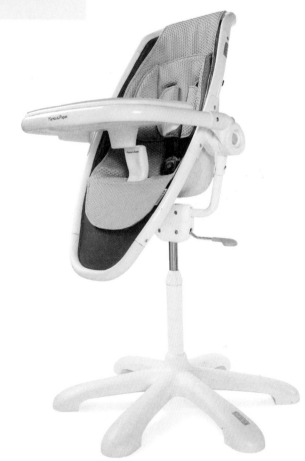

Proportional analysis

Concept cars seen at motor shows usually have good proportions because their visual impact is so important. Some are given extreme proportions to make them stand out. As these concepts move towards production, the proportions are often adjusted for practicality or to reduce cost. This can compromise the styling, resulting in a less visually appealing product. That is why it is critical for designers to collaborate closely with the engineering team at the start of a project, before the hard points become fixed. The vehicles in **fig. 3.14** demonstrate the proportional differences between a concept car and the production version. The changes may seem trivial, but the effect is dramatic. The concept car at the top is well proportioned, with a perfect three-wheel-space wheelbase (pink circles), and the rear window relates to the rear wheel arch (light blue line). The proportions of the production car below are slightly different. The wheelbase is a little shorter than that of the concept, which has the effect of shifting the rear wheel inwards, resulting in a heavier-looking rear end and misaligned window. This decision may have been made to increase boot space or as a cost-cutting measure that allowed the company to use an existing platform instead of engineering a new one.

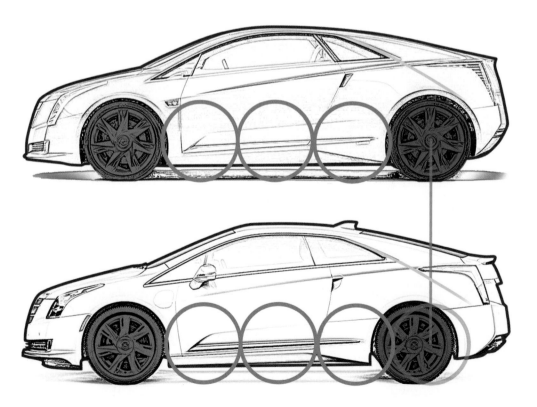

3.14 Cadillac Converj concept car, 2009, and Cadillac ELR production car, 2013: illustrating the proportional differences between a concept car and the production version

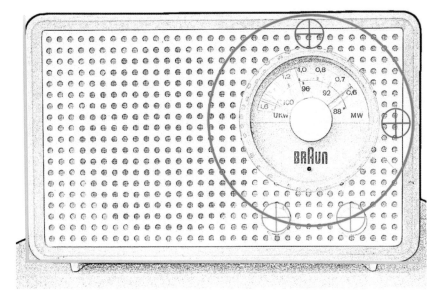

3.15 Braun SK2 radio, 1952. Below, the thought behind the visual design: Golden Ratio outer case, and carefully planned size and position of dial and controls

In the twentieth century Dieter Rams and his team at Braun designed products that focused on simplicity, ease of use and good proportions. He became renowned for designing products with a functionalist style influenced by the Bauhaus movement, and his designs are still influencing many products in the twenty-first century – proof that simple shapes and good proportions can be all that is required to create an appealing product.

The length of the radio in **fig. 3.15** is 0.618 times greater than its height (blue lines), meaning that its silhouette conforms to the Golden Ratio. The space between the dial and the edge of the case matches the diameter of the control knobs below it, and the control knobs are

positioned on an imaginary circle (pink) that is tangential with the case, relating them to the dial and case. It is an innovative way of creating visual harmony.

The watch is another product in which proportion has a huge effect on the final appearance, and also how it looks, proportionally, on a wrist of a particular size. These two examples use chronograph dials to provide different visual results.

The watch at **fig. 3.16** uses two chronograph dial sizes. The pink and orange chronograph dial diameters have been influenced by the day/date window (dark blue), which has been sized to meet the edge of the watch (green) when duplicated. The light blue dial doesn't quite meet the edge of the watch when duplicated, which may be why this dial has been designed to blend in with the main watch face. The pink and orange dials, however, are the correct diameter to meet the edge of the watch when duplicated. So they have been designed to draw your eye with a metallic border resulting in a complex but harmonious design.

3.16 Based closely on the TAG Heuer Carrera Calibre 16 Day-Date watch, 2008 to current, this model uses a metallic feature to draw the eye to the better proportioned chronograph dial

The watch at **fig. 3.17** uses only one dial size and is organized slightly differently. The dials are very close together, adding visual tension, and when duplicated are very close to meeting the edge of the watch (green). Note also that the horizontal gap between the left and right dials is exactly half a dial long (light blue). The indices have been neatly placed around the dials to provide a harmonious link (dark blue).

If you cannot achieve ideal proportions because of engineering constraints, there are other styling techniques that can help to mask undesirable proportions. Once you are confident creating silhouettes and proportions, you can begin designing them simultaneously.

3.17 Based closely on the Omega Speedmaster watch, 1957 to current, this model has closely spaced chronograph dials that add visual tension

Chapter overview

Critique the product's current proportions and improve details that are unevenly spaced or unrelated. Could more extreme proportions help the product to stand out among the competition? Are there any features that could be enlarged to highlight their visual importance?

01 | **Be aware of current proportional trends in that particular product category, and either replicate or avoid them.**

02 | **Would the product benefit from being more slender, and how could that be achieved?**

03 | **Has the spacing of the major visual features been optimized? The connection between a feature's scale and position and its relationship to the product silhouette are critical to its appearance.**

04 | **Reducing a product's height can increase its perceived width, and in the same way lengthening a silhouette can visually reduce its width. Make sure the ergonomics do not suffer as a result of such adjustments, however.**

05 | **A product with a bland rectangular silhouette, such as an external hard drive, may benefit from having proportions that adhere to the Golden Ratio.**

06 | **If the silhouette has several points, make sure they are horizontally or vertically aligned with other points or visual features.**

Case study:
Electric Kettle

The kettle's overall proportions have remained the same as the benchmark kettle seen in the previous chapter (see page 39). Because it has few major visual features in this 2D view (water-level indicator, lid and base), the designer has instead focused on the silhouette's proportional alignments. It has been designed so that most visual points intersect horizontally or vertically with neighbouring points (pink dots), making the design appear balanced.

For example, the tip of the spout is aligned horizontally with the inside arc of the handle, and the water-level indicator is parallel to the lower rear body of the silhouette, all of which creates a more harmonious appearance. With practice you will be able to do this instinctively, without having to add a grid.

Original design

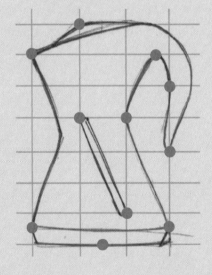

Remember, if a product doesn't look quite right it is usually because of proportional imperfections, so take time to get this stage right.

Revised design

Chapter 4

Shape

Learning objectives

- Define shape in relation to a product (page 60).

- Recognize the symbolism and meaning associated with different shapes (page 62).

- Explain how to design a new shape (page 63).

- Discuss the relationship between intersecting lines and shape (page 64).

- Explain how symbolism can be incorporated into a product's shape (page 66).

- Define shape cloning (page 67).

- Identify the factors that contribute to the dynamism of a shape (page 68).

- Discuss the relationship between pattern and shape (page 69).

- Summarize the main points of shape design (page 70).

Chapter 4
Shape

Shape describes the 2D form of the visual features found in a silhouette. Most products have functional visual features (such as a digital display, user controls, a handle), and these shapes have been optimized for specific functional, ergonomic or visual reasons. Stylistically neglected shapes or those with undesirable symbolism may affect the overall visual quality of the product.

Shapes add character and meaning (semiotics) to products through their visual symbolism and association, which in turn affect perception of the product. This meaning can be superficial or it can be designed to improve first-time use, especially when shapes with similar functions are grouped together logically.

There are two types of shape: solid and empty. The shapes seen on these two pages are solid shapes. Empty shapes are those that are hollow, such as the handle of a kettle or the ventilation ducts on a laptop. Shapes that mirror the product's silhouette tend to look most harmonious. For instance, if a silhouette has a rounded form, its visual features would ideally also be round, assuming circles meet the functional requirements and chosen theme. The circular shapes seen on the baby monitor in **fig. 4.1** echo its rounded silhouette, while exuding friendliness and softness – the perfect choice for a product aimed at the new baby category.

If the brief is to design a conservative aesthetic that will blend in to its environment, self-control and a careful selection of shape will be required from the designer. The examples that follow have shapes that provide differing visual information.

> '**Simplicity is the key to excellence.**'
>
> **Dieter Rams, product designer**

4.1 Tomy Ecoute TF525 digital baby monitor, 2013

4.2 Brother HL-2240D laser printer, 2010

The design of the printer (**fig. 4.2**) involves simple rectangular shapes that echo its silhouette. This product is designed to be unobtrusive and blend in to its environment, which are desirable traits for some consumers.

The shapes on the computer mouse (**fig. 4.3**) are organic in style, which suggests that it will fit comfortably in the hand. This is a very important element of shape styling. If a shape is to be handled or operated by a user, it must appear inviting to touch. When sketching concepts it is fine to style angular products, but the areas where human interaction take place should be designed more sensitively to ensure the customer will not feel discomfort when using the product for long periods.

4.3 Logitech MX Master 3 mouse, 2019

It is possible to improve functional shapes that are visually undesirable or too predictable. Take an empty shape such as the handle of a kettle. Once the basic shape and ergonomic hard points have been determined, the designer can decide which of the lines could be modified without impeding function. Another option might be to inject into the design an appropriate symbolic shape that matches those hard points, as demonstrated in the silhouette stage (Chapter 2).

Shapes can be very expressive, and associations will be made quickly by the viewer. Shapes should always be influenced by function, and then styled (if required) using influences taken from the original mood board. Shape design can also influence the implied gender of a product. Softer shapes can suggest a more feminine product (**fig. 4.4**), and more angular shapes are often associated with more masculine products. However, this can vary depending on the customer and product category.

4.4 Gillette Venus Spa Breeze razor, 2008, with a softer shape than razors aimed at men

Consistency and coherence of shape

Throughout its design, the baby monitor in fig. 4.1 uses ellipses (highlighted in pink in **fig. 4.5**) that blend with the overall form and surfacing. It is important to create coherent shapes that are in touch with the overall product form language to achieve a more harmonious result. The most common 2D shapes found in product design are based on simple geometry, such as circles and ellipses. Streamlined shapes, such as teardrops, have also proven effective at highlighting the performance aspects of products. Using recognizable symbolic shapes is an efficient way to portray meaning or evoke emotional reactions in viewers, who are more likely to connect subconsciously with those shapes. Alternatively, innovative shapes can create a more distinctive or modern appearance.

4.5 The Tomy baby monitor uses consistent shapes throughout

The classic luxury watch in **fig. 4.6** was designed by the Swiss watch designer Gérald Genta. The polygonal shapes throughout its design – octagonal bezel, hexagonal screws and crown – were an innovative way to create visual distinction in its day. The design is said to have been inspired by a 1970s diving helmet. Although the helmet is not polygonal, the exposed rivets around the viewing window were clearly an influence.

4.6 Left, Audemars Piguet Royal Oak men's watch, 1972–present. Right, deep-sea diving helmet inspiration

Designing new shapes

Designing a shape is similar to designing a silhouette, but association and symbolism play a much more important role in shape because they are more apparent. First, confirm that a functional shape can be modified without affecting the use or ergonomics of the product. Assuming that the functional shape needs improving, select a suitable and relevant shape that matches the original theme. This shape can then be abstracted to simplify its form. The aim is to give the viewer a taste of the original shape; it should not be too obvious where it was derived from.

 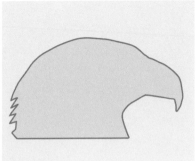 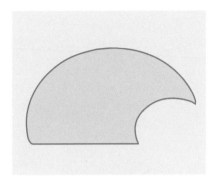

Fig. 4.7 shows an example of how to design a new shape with symbolism and association. Here, we start with the head of an eagle to create a shape that will evoke speed and agility. The outline is abstracted to achieve the final feature shape.

4.7 New shape design to evoke speed and agility

Designing with intersecting shapes

It's important to demonstrate an example of more complex shape design, often seen in the automotive sector, since this method can result in ideal continuity of appearance across a product and its visual features.

Intersections are created when several lines converge on the surface of a product. The design of the headlight shape in **fig. 4.8** (pink) is the result of an intersection of neighbouring lines: the second wheel-arch line (orange), the bonnet shut lines (blue) and the top of the grille. (Shut lines are formed when two neighbouring components meet; see page 87.)

4.8 Mazda Kabura concept car, 2006, with shapes influenced by intersecting lines

This technique of using line intersections results in a visually optimal headlight shape that harmonizes with the surrounding features. The designers have shown a lot of restraint; the only bit of design flair seen in the headlight shape is the 'frowning' top line that flows from the front bonnet shut line into the second wheel-arch surface crease, and it adds character. This illustrates that if there will be several converging lines on the form of a product, it may be best to allow the intersections to influence the design of the shapes.

Once a new shape has been sketched lightly into position, its proportions and angle can be adjusted if necessary to achieve the best visual result.

When styling in two dimensions, keep in mind that shapes positioned on the edges of a silhouette may have depth, and therefore may wrap around the side of the product. This means that a shape viewed in side profile may also be visible when seen from the front or back of the product, and must therefore also look right in those views. Look at the shapes of the front air inlets in the 2D view in **fig. 4.9**. Moving around the helmet, the shapes change as they wrap around it. This is why it is necessary to design the other 2D product views to ensure all the visual features will blend harmoniously, before moving into three dimensions.

Intersections are created when several lines converge on the surface of a product. Optimal shapes can be designed with these intersections.

4.9 Abus Tec-Tical 2.1 cycle helmet, 2018: shape transition from side to front view

Chapter Four | Shape

Shape semiotics

Semiotics is the study of signs and symbols and how we interpret them. It can be very useful when designing shapes that are to be interacted with, to improve the ease of first-time use for a customer. Observe the car door panel in **fig. 4.10**. There are three key elements that deserve focus here in terms of shape design. The first is the well-known seat shape found in the centre of the panel. It is an abstracted seat profile, but we immediately understand what this feature will do if we interact with it. The second shape of interest is the door-release handle, which has a horn-like pointed shape. This is the most important feature on the entire door panel, as it is the only one that might be needed in an emergency. The shape has obviously been designed for comfort and efficiency, but its sharpness perhaps helps to draw the eye to it, making it stand out among the softer neighbouring shapes. The third shape of interest is the white door handle, a soft, organic shape designed for comfort.

These designs demonstrate that shapes have psychological meaning that designers can use to influence a customer's interaction with their products. Sharp shapes catch our eye owing to their potential to harm us, while soft shapes appear more tactile and encourage interaction.

4.10 Mercedes-Benz S500 Coupé, 2018, shape semiotics of interior door panel

Observe the remote control in **fig. 4.11**. The first button that draws the eye is the large, circular, light grey one in the centre, so this should logically be the power button, the first point of contact. The size and colour of shapes can improve the ease of first-time use, and should be considered during shape styling. The buttons that are most frequently used (channel and volume) are separated visually by the large black shape, which makes them easy to find. It's interesting that the designer has chosen a shape that resembles a propeller for this product, as there is no obvious reason for it. However, using this familiar shape is a neat way of disguising an otherwise boxy silhouette. The various buttons are grouped logically according to their function, for ease of use.

4.11 URC R50 remote control, 2004

4.12 Morphy Richards 43820 kettle, 2011 (modified image)

Shape cloning

Cloning is when a functional shape is copied and scaled to fit around the original shape. This creates impact and draws attention to the area. The designer of the kettle in **fig. 4.12** has made an attractive visual feature of the handle opening by incorporating an organic teardrop shape. This empty shape has been cloned by the shut line (pink) that surrounds it (see page 87 for shut lines). In this case it is not an exact replica of the original, but it is clearly related, and the contrasting colour makes it stand out. The designer has accentuated the teardrop by cloning it once again in the outer edge of the panel (green). Our eyes would have been drawn to this design detail had it been given a contrasting colour. Styling is as much about reducing unattractiveness as it is about enhancing good looks.

 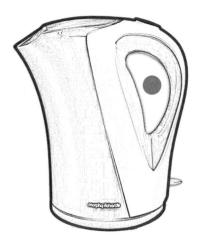

4.13 Left, offset handle hole. Right, centred handle hole

It may be difficult to spot the subtle differences in **fig. 4.13**, but the opening of the kettle handle on the left looks slightly more dynamic than the one on the right, owing to a slight offset between the shapes. The left handle opening is positioned to the upper left of the handle area, towards the pink dot. The handle opening on the right has been centred so that it appears more balanced and static. Try offsetting a dominant shape to increase impact.

Shape dynamics

There is a big difference visually between the vertical and the angled handle guard on the drill seen in **fig. 4.14**. Bosch angled and tapered this feature for greater visual impact.

4.14 The Bosch PBH 2100 RE electric drill, 2012. Left, the original design: right, with a vertical, less dynamic handle shape

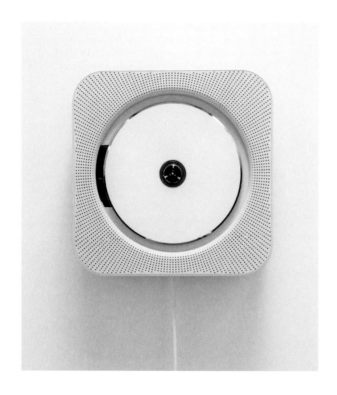

Patterns

When several shapes are repeated and arranged in a consistent manner, a pattern is formed. For a pattern to complement a design, it should relate to the surrounding visual features or silhouette. In **fig. 4.15**, the concentric pattern of the speaker holes relates to the circular volume that houses the CD, resulting in a harmonious appearance.

Once the shapes have been optimized, some products may not require additional visual elaboration, other than functional shut lines (see page 87). It is possible to design attractive products with these three simple styling stages: silhouette, proportion and shape. Since these designs will look fairly simple, the details will be even more important, so double-check that the proportions are optimized and that the alignment of the visual features makes functional and visual sense. When it comes to the modelling stage, ensure that radii or chamfers are as consistent as possible throughout (e.g. 1mm radius and 45-degree chamfer), for a harmonious design.

The chosen 2D view should now appear in equilibrium. You should not feel that any visual features require major repositioning, rescaling or restyling. If there are surfaces that need consideration, Chapter 8 will provide guidance.

4.15 Muji wall-mounted CD player, 1999, with radially patterned speaker holes. On the right, with highlighted concentric hole pattern that complements the CD

If you feel that more visual information is required to make the design look less generic, the following stages will provide further options for styling development. This is also a good place to complete the other 2D views that will be required to move the product accurately into three dimensions (see Chapter 9). **Fig. 4.16** shows a General Arrangement drawing (GA) that illustrates the various 2D views of a camera. Decide which views will be required to take the design forward into three dimensions; front, side and top views are most commonly used.

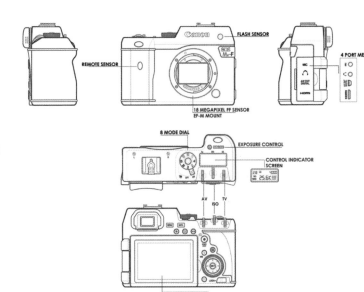

4.16 Canon digital camera GA showing several 2D views

Chapter overview

Critique the shapes of the product's visual features sketched earlier. If modifications are required, sketch some designs separately before injecting them into the product, and consider the following:

01	**If a product is likely to need several functional or character lines, design them alongside the shapes (see Chapter 6). In many cases the most suitable shapes are those that are formed by intersecting lines.**
02	**Is it possible to relate the shapes to the silhouette?**
03	**Shapes should be first influenced by function and then styled, if required, using influences taken from the original mood board.**
04	**If an undesirable shape is found, decide which edges could be modified without affecting the function, and try some alternatives.**
05	**Shapes also have psychological meaning (semiotics) that designers can use to influence the customer's interaction with their products. Does the chosen shape encourage or discourage interaction?**
06	**If a product has several buttons or controls, it is wise to group them by function, shape, size and colour to improve ease of use.**

Case study:
Electric Kettle

The only shape that needed modifying in this case was the water-level indicator, which looked out of place due to a lack of visual relation to the surrounding features. It was repositioned to be in line with the upper body where it meets the handle, as seen below.

This shape is modified slightly in the following chapters as the design develops.

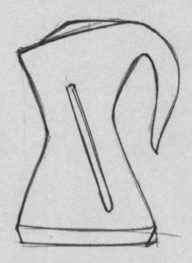

Original design

The water-level indicator was repositioned to improve visual relationships.

Revised design

Chapter 5

Stance

Learning objectives

- Define the term 'stance' in relation to a product (page 74).

- Explain how inspiration for a product's stance can be taken from nature (page 75).

- Identify different types of stance: dynamic, solid and gestural (pages 75–78).

- Experiment by applying different types of stance to a single product (page 79).

- Summarize the main points of stance design (page 78).

Chapter 5
Stance

The term 'stance' describes the posture of a product. You may wish to emphasize a product's stance to add character or impact, as a way of increasing the expressiveness of its design language. Imagine a sprinter waiting in the 'set' position at the start of a race (**fig. 5.1**). It is a dynamic position, with legs ready to spring into action, weight shifted to the front, and arms supporting the pent-up motion. These distinctive visual characteristics can be injected into a product in several ways.

- Dynamic stance

- Solid stance

- Gestural stance

'I think it's really important to design things with a kind of personality.'

Marc Newson, product designer

5.1 Athlete's dynamic stance

Dynamic stance

A dynamic stance can be achieved by simply shifting the weight of a product to one side. This creates the illusion that the product is off balance and about to move, which adds visual tension. Changing the stance of a design will obviously require modifications to its silhouette and functional features, so consult the package drawing if possible to ensure these changes can be accommodated. The kettle in **fig. 5.2** gets its dynamic appearance from its angled stance and tapering silhouette. The right-angled triangle was chosen to add dynamism to the handle's empty shape.

When the cheetah is ready to pounce (**fig. 5.3**), it raises its rear off the ground and lowers its head, which shifts its weight on to its front legs and gives it pent-up forward motion.

5.2 Bugatti Vera kettle, 2015, dynamic stance

5.3 The dynamic stance of the cheetah

Chapter Five | Stance

The product designer can create a similar stance using the following techniques, seen on the computer mouse in **fig. 5.4**:

5.4 Logitech MX Anywhere 2 mouse, 2015, dynamic stance

1. The designer has raised the rear of the silhouette (on the right) above the front, to create pent-up forward motion and dynamism.

2. There are no horizontal lines or shapes in the design; all are angled, to complement and enhance the dynamic silhouette. The lines sweep gracefully from front to back.

3. The lines at the bottom of the product create an arc that has the visual effect of lifting the belly of the mouse off the ground. This mimics the back of the cheetah's stance, where the arc is between the bottom of the ribcage and the hind legs. Designers pick out such nuances from images found in the mood board, and use them in their designs to achieve a similar feel. It is easier to transfer these elements if you select a subject that has similar proportions to the designed object.

Select a stance that will add value to the user. It's possible to increase a product's visual efficiency with references to speed, giving the impression that a task will be completed more quickly. Adding a solid stance can increase a product's visual robustness.

Solid stance

The piglet (**fig. 5.5**) has a solid stance, owing to its stable form and equally distributed weight. Elements of the stance of the toaster in **fig. 5.6** resemble that of the piglet. Its weight is evenly distributed between its four feet, which are at its edges, giving it a stocky appearance that increases the impression of stability and weight. Whether intentional or not, the rounded form, colour and circular control at the front add to the toaster's cuteness and its resemblance to a pig.

Chapter Five Stance

5.6 Smeg two-slice toaster, 2015

Gestural stance

The Anglepoise lamp (**fig. 5.7**) was designed by George Carwardine in the 1930s to allow for maximum adjustability for the user. Its functional form has a stance that evokes a person bending down, providing a gestural human likeness that adds character and makes it look distinctive.

5.7 The Anglepoise+Paul Smith Type 75 Mini lamp, 2014, has a gestural stance

Chapter overview

A designer may wish to emphasize a product's stance to add character or visual impact, ensuring that the design will stand out among the competition.

01 | **What is the most important visual characteristic to communicate to the customer?**

02 | **Would the concept benefit from the extra character and visual impact offered by a change of stance?**

03 | **Choose an image of a stance that reflects the desired visual qualities or emotions, and dissect the elements that give it its character.**

Case study:
Electric Kettle

The first kettle design (at the top) has a solid, static stance. If a more dynamic stance were desired, the silhouette could simply be tilted, as seen on the version below. The weight has been shifted to the front, and the designer has also started to experiment with the styling of the base and handle.

Original design

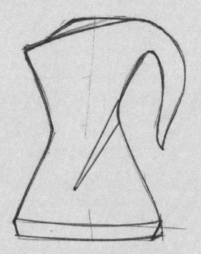

Static stance above, and below with a more dynamic stance.

Revised design

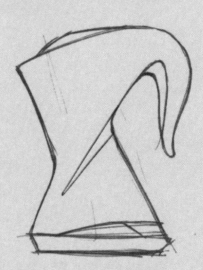

Chapter 6

Lines

Learning objectives

- Define the term 'lines' in relation to a product (page 82).

- Discuss lines and how they relate to a product's other visual features (page 84).

- List the different types of line relationship: collinear, tangent, on centre, on point (page 84).

- Explain tapering and how it is used to increase visual dynamism (page 85).

- Experiment with adjusting lines on an existing product (page 86).

- Identify the following line types: shut lines, surface crease lines, solid shape lines, empty shape lines, graphic lines (pages 87–90).

- Summarize the main points of using lines in design (page 90).

Chapter 6

Lines

Once you are confident in your well-proportioned 2D view, the next step is to decide if the product will require any functional lines (such as shut lines, where two components meet) and, if so, how they can be designed to enhance or blend in to the design. You may decide to add visual lines purely for emotion or character, but not all products need elaboration in this way, and the functional elements or stance may provide enough distinction. Products without character lines can appear generic, and may fail to stand out among the competition. This is where the designer's flair and creativity can come into play, but it is important that new lines consistently reflect the chosen theme. Also bear in mind that if the competition is using a particular design language, it may be best to design a new direction to guarantee distinctiveness – as long as it is in line with the customer's aspirations.

Functional lines are common in products that have more than one component in their exterior assembly. Shut lines appear when two or more components are assembled, as seen in **fig. 6.1**, where the purple panel meets the white panel. This line has been styled to complement the silhouette. If it were an angular line, for instance, the product would not be so elegant.

Innovation is important in the design of character lines, since that is where most self-expression is possible. Distinctive lines can be designed only with experimentation

'A watch should appear precise, a car should appear agile.'

Del Coates, designer and author

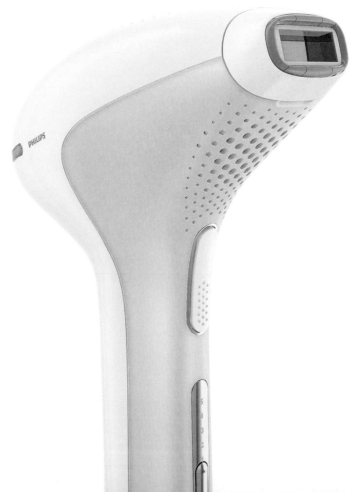

6.1 Philips Lumea IPL hair remover, 2009

and freedom of expression. Some designers like to sketch quick, random lines across a silhouette to find inspiration; among the resulting chaos they will spot an area of interest and develop it. An element of restraint is necessary when selecting lines, because over-elaboration or fussy styling may result in a less appealing product.

Lines sketched in two dimensions run in one direction or plane, but it is important to remember that sometimes lines flow across a three-dimensional (3D) form in more than one plane. In other words, a line may look straight when viewed from the side, but when seen from above it may take a different path as it follows the 3D form. The helmet's top lines have curvature when viewed in side profile (turquoise), but these same lines also have curvature in another plane when seen from above, as they follow the contours of the 3D form (**fig. 6.2**).

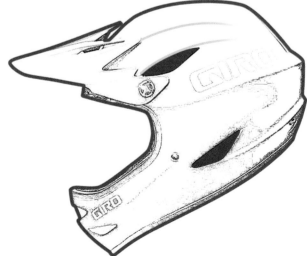

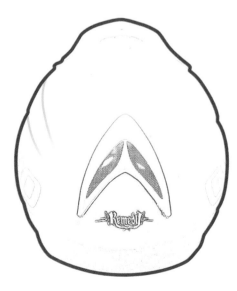

6.2 Giro Remedy helmet, 2013. Below, showing lines curving in different planes

Visual continuity and relation

To achieve visual continuity across a product, lines should relate to neighbouring visual features or other lines in the chosen view. The design will look more harmonious if lines have a clear and logical start and end point. The surface crease line seen in **fig. 6.3** starts its journey around the rotary button and ends at the comb. This line has purposeful direction, appearing heavier at the start and lighter at the end, which adds visual energy. This effect is created by varying the surface depth of the line in cross-section, thus altering the size of the shadow beneath it.

Angled lines can make a product look less static. They add visual energy while also enhancing the stance. Purely horizontal or vertical lines are useful for giving an impression of strength and solidity, and for products that are required to blend in to their environments.

It is common for lines to begin or end with the following feature relations: collinear, tangent, on centre or on point (**fig. 6.4**). Lines that sweep along the length of a product can also make it seem longer, which is a useful trick when dealing with proportionally short-looking products that would look better if they had more length.

6.3 Remington Barba Beard Trimmer, 2015

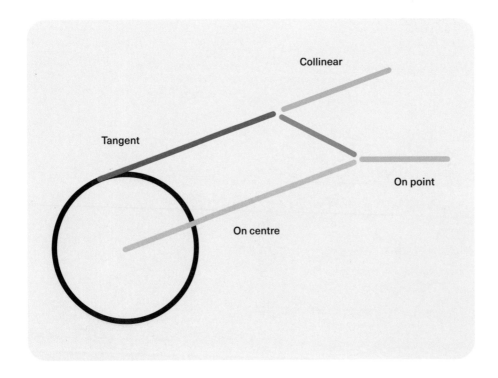

6.4 Common line relations to visual features

Tapering

Another effective dynamic technique is to add taper between two lines. Tapering – when two neighbouring lines gradually move closer to each other at one end – adds grace and dynamism. Observe the tapering surfaces in **fig. 6.5**, formed by carefully placed lines that create maximum visual impact. Line tapering can also create visual tension in surfaces (see Chapter 8). Tapering is one of the keys to dynamic and sensual product styling, and is often found in nature's more beautiful creations.

The Panton chair acquires its elegance from gracefully tapering lines and voluptuous surfaces. If the tapering at the side of the chair is reduced, so is the visual elegance. Spot the difference in **fig. 6.6**.

6.5 Philips PerfectCare Elite Plus steam iron GC9660/36

6.6 Panton Classic, 1967. On the right, less tapering means less elegance

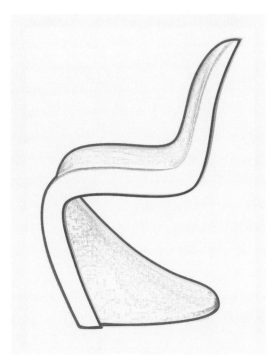

Line design

Sketch some lines lightly across the silhouette of the product, ensuring that they relate to other design features. Try adding slight curvature to those lines (unless function dictates otherwise). Line curvature should come naturally by pivoting the pen through the wrist or forearm. Be bold and allow the lines to go past the silhouette for now (the excess can be erased later if you wish), to ensure they have natural continuity and dynamism. Experiment by connecting lines with the visual features created earlier, to add relation (collinear, tangent, central or on point). Try making minor adjustments to some of the visual feature edges to see if the relationship between them and the character lines can be improved. The kettle sketch on the left of **fig. 6.7** shows how the designer has experimented by ghosting faint lines to test different options. Once the preferred solution is found, the chosen lines are darkened to improve contrast. Note that the shape of the handle hole on the left is less appealing than the neater design on the right, which has been redrawn.

 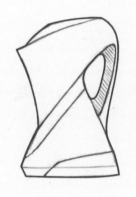

6.7 Left, line experimentation. Right, chosen lines

6.8 Common line relations to visual features

While sketching, try to work out the purpose of each line and how it will work best with the product (see **fig. 6.8**). Lines can be applied to products in the following combinations.

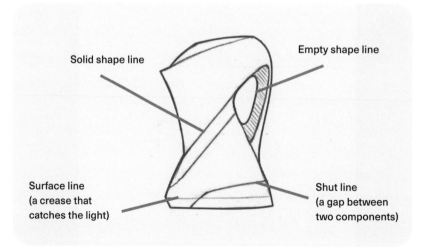

Solid shape line

Empty shape line

Surface line (a crease that catches the light)

Shut line (a gap between two components)

Shut lines

Sketched lines will become shut lines where two neighbouring components meet, or where clearance is required to allow a panel to open or a button to move; see the pink lines in **fig. 6.9**.

When plastic parts that fit together are manufactured, production tolerance variation means that they can be slightly larger or smaller than their exact specification. Engineers ensure that when a component has to fit within another (such as a door into a frame), assembly will be possible even when the part that is to be inserted (the door) is at its largest and the part that houses it (the frame) is at its smallest. Clearance is required to account for this variation, and that is why shut lines appear as dark lines, because the area beyond the gap is in shadow (**fig. 6.10**). Although these lines are functional, it is still important to make them work visually with the whole design.

6.9 Sony PlayStation DualShock 4 Controller, 2016, with shut lines highlighted

6.10 BMW Motorrad AirFlow helmet, 2017, with shut lines highlighted

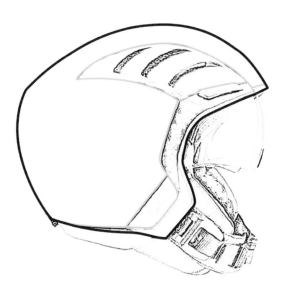

When it comes to the physical 3D modelling stage, some designers apply a black marker or thin black masking tape to their models to experiment with and perfect the design of the shut lines. This ensures that the shut lines will flow around the 3D form in the most satisfying manner possible.

Surface crease lines

Surface creases appear at the intersection of two opposing surfaces (see purple lines at **fig. 6.11**, and Chapter 8). Designers create these lines to add character and dynamism to their products. A 'line' becomes visible when light reflects off the surfaces at different angles, leaving one side darker than the other. Light can also catch the crease itself, forming a bright highlight that draws the eye. The design of surface creases is often optimized during the 3D modelling stage.

Note how the surface creases (highlighted) extend past the silver components in fig. 6.11 to improve line continuity across the product. This works visually even though one 'line' is an edge of a solid shape and the other is a surface crease. Designers use these different kinds of line while sketching to improve visual continuity and work out how the product will be manufactured.

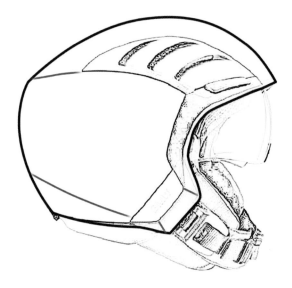

6.11 BMW Motorrad AirFlow helmet, 2017. On the right, with surface crease lines highlighted

 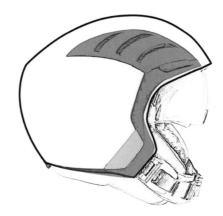

6.12 BMW Motorrad AirFlow helmet, 2017. On the right, with solid shapes highlighted

Solid shape lines

Sketched lines can sometimes become solid shapes. The shapes highlighted in **fig. 6.12** are separate components that have been assembled on the helmet, which is why shut lines are visible around them. Shapes and lines often influence each other, since the designer's goal is to make them relate to each other visually. It's common to see the edges of solid shapes flowing into other types of line, to improve line continuity. It is possible that the shape above, with the three inlet slots, started life on the designer's page as a single line, and that it was decided to make a feature of the slots by encapsulating them in the horn-like shape highlighted in purple.

Empty shape lines

The air-intake cavities highlighted in **fig. 6.13** are functional, guiding air to demist the flip-down visor. Non-functional cavities are sometimes added to products to create visual interest or to improve the continuity of the lines. If adding a cavity to a design is not an option and more styling details are required, it may be possible to design a solid shape that is embossed into the surface purely as a styling aid.

Chapter Six | Lines

6.13 BMW Motorrad AirFlow helmet, 2017. On the right, with empty shapes highlighted

Graphics

The final type of line that can be used in product design is simply a change of colour. Painted areas or graphics can enhance the dynamics of a product when physical lines are not suitable. Lines can be formed by the graphic design themselves, as illustrated by the red lines in **fig. 6.14**. Lines can also appear when two contrasting coloured graphics meet. Graphics can be applied in many ways, including water-transfer printing, tampo printing (tampography or pad printing) and vinyl stickers. They are often used for branding, but can also be used to improve line continuity or dynamism, as seen here.

6.14 Mercury Marine 250hp V8 Pro XS
outboard motor, 2019, with red line graphics

Chapter overview

Lines add emotion and character. The designer's creativity can come into play, but it's important that new lines are linked to the chosen theme.

01   **Do the lines begin and end with the following feature relations: collinear, tangent, central or on point?**

02   **Sometimes the most suitable shape designs are those that simply intersect lines. Could the shapes of the visual features be tweaked to improve line flow and relation?**

03   **An element of restraint is necessary when selecting lines, since over-elaboration or fussy styling can result in a less attractive product.**

04   **Lines that are angled from the horizontal can give a design dynamism and motion, while also enhancing the stance. Is it appropriate or feasible to angle the lines?**

05   **Tapered neighbouring lines are one of the keys to attractive and dynamic styling. Is there scope to incorporate these into the design?**

06   **Try adding a slight curve to the lines for a more natural and emotional design.**

07   **Sketched lines can be applied to a design in the following ways: shut lines, surface creases, solid shapes, empty shapes, graphics.**

Case study: Electric Kettle

The sketch above right looks messy, because the designer has been experimenting with line and shape. The water-level indicator is an important visual feature that has been extended across the side of the body, so that it relates to the handle and the silhouette. The designer has also decided to merge the handle back into the body, instead of leaving the end exposed, which creates an empty shape that has been tweaked to intersect with the surrounding lines neatly. Another concept with an unconnected handle could easily be designed as a secondary option.

The completed side profile (below) has been resketched by overlaying the original to make it more presentable. The silhouette was then darkened to make it stand out.

Original design

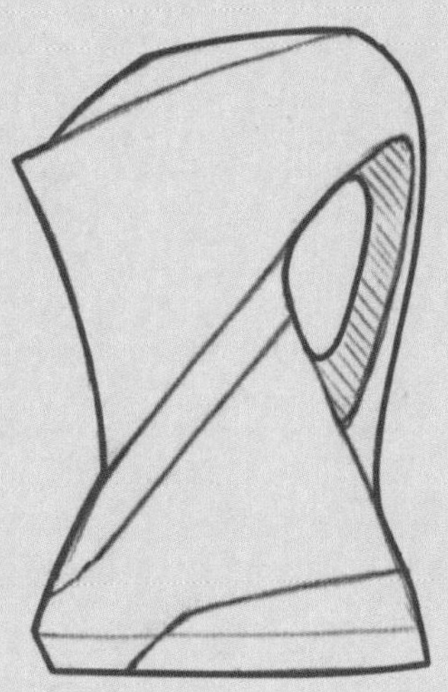

Revised design

Having completed this chapter, it may be worth reviewing the silhouette of your product to see if any minor adjustments could be made to improve its relationship to the lines you have added.

Chapter 7

Volume

Learning objectives

- Define the term 'volume' in relation to a product (page 94).

- Explain how to change the appearance of an existing product's volume (page 94).

- Demonstrate how to break up volumes to reduce bulk (page 97).

- Summarize the main points of volume design (page 98).

Chapter 7
Volume

Some parts of a design can look dull or overpowering owing to large volumes that lack visual information. A volume is a clearly defined shape or area of a 3D product that is either solid or empty. The handle hole seen in **fig. 7.1** is a volume that has been visually considered, even though it is empty. By splitting undesirably large volumes into smaller bodies, you can achieve a more slender and interesting appearance.

The handle and three triangular grey volumes (speaker and controls) of the radio in fig. 7.1 help to separate the main black volume into multiples, which gives the illusion of a slimmer, and therefore lighter, product. If the main volume were red, for example, the volume separation would become even more pronounced. This product is designed to be carried around in emergencies, so it's important that it should appear lightweight but also robust.

Introducing new volumes

Volumes are often bound by function, and so may not be easy to manipulate. If a solid volume looks dull or undesirably heavy, it may be possible to add another volume to it by simply cloning its profile as a solid or empty shape, which will increase visual separation.

Fig. 7.2 shows an infant carrier concept in side profile, with the main volumes highlighted in different colours. The main lower volume (pink) looked heavy before a smaller volume (orange) was added to echo it. This orange volume has the added benefit of helping the surrounding lines and surfaces to flow more gracefully. The main headrest volume (purple) is separated visually from the lower main volume (pink), as the surface twists and dips inwards at the intersection. Note that it also complements the main volume, because it mirrors its shape.

7.1 Etón FRX5 Sidekick digital radio, 2019

7.2 Infant carrier concept, 2008, with main volumes highlighted

Fig. 7.3 shows the result of cloning a volume. The large lower volume has been echoed inwards as a hole in the side.

It is not always functionally viable to lighten a volume visually by removing sections from it. It is more common for designers to add solid volumes to improve visual separation, and these often come in the form of additional functional components or shapes.

The conservative-looking PC on the left of **fig. 7.4** looks plain because of its lack of visual information and its boxy silhouette. In the second design, the equally boxy silhouette is disguised with a curved silver volume that draws the eye away from the silhouette's straight edges. In the third design, shapes and details increase volume separation, adding distinction and lightening the design visually.

7.3 Infant carrier concept, 2008, without (top image) and with additional volume

7.4 PCs with different form language and volume division. Left: unstyled PC, centre: Arctic Cooling Silentium Eco-80, 2002, right: Dell Precision T7500

Chapter Seven Volume

7.5 Dell Inspiron 5680
Gaming Desktop PC, 2018

7.6 Philips Saeco coffee machine,
2010

The designer of the PC in **fig. 7.5** has split the form asymmetrically into two volumes by making a visual feature of the diagonal cooling ducts. Asymmetrical products tend to be less visually appealing, but in this case the design is more striking than those in fig. 7.4 because our eyes are not used to the form. Asymmetry is worth experimenting with, depending on the preferences of the target market.

The designer of the coffee maker in **fig. 7.6** has added organic volumes to break up the form. These have been transformed into flowing surfaces that may be designed to emulate liquid coffee.

Many vehicles have large rear volumes, so designers split them into smaller volumes to reduce visual bulk and add interest. The rear of the car in **fig. 7.7** divides into four main volumes (below right). The heights of the pink, yellow and green volumes are roughly the same (rule of thirds) and match the height from the ground to the lower bumper. The

7.7 Volvo XC coupé concept,
2014. Right, with rear volume
divisions highlighted

additional height of the rear window is close to 0.618 times the height of the other volumes (Golden Ratio). The shape of the lights, exhausts, number plate and rear diffuser all add visual separation and character. Without these divisions, the rear would look bulky and unappealing.

Volume design

When critiquing a product's volumes, first highlight areas that could be improved visually. Several options are available to reduce the visual bulk of these areas. The shape of the original volume can be cloned inwards, creating a smaller volume that is in harmony with the original. New details, such as shapes or lines, can be added to increase visual separation, and surface volumes can be manipulated to improve visual separation (see Chapter 8).

Having completed this stage, you should be content with the styling of the chosen 2D view. If not, work through the styling stages again in more detail, or select another visual theme that may suit the product better.

Creating a range of styling options

In order to select the best concept, and increase the likelihood of meeting the client's requirements, the designer must create several styling options. It is unlikely that the first attempt will be the best one, so creating many concepts quickly is a valuable skill. To produce a range of inspiring styling options, you can innovate in the following areas:

1. **Functionality and ergonomics**

2. **A completely new visual theme and form language**

3. **Using Osborn's Checklist for inspiration (see page 13)**

4. **Omitting one or more of the styling stages to achieve a different aesthetic**

This may also be a good opportunity to try any personal styling ideas that have come to mind while reading this book. Challenge yourself to design a minimum of ten different options for each product.

When you are presenting concepts, the client may expect to see several views of each design, for more information, and 3D views are also desirable (see Chapter 9). To provide a representative 3D view,

> '**Establish a perfect balance of the masses, ensuring that all volumes are where they need to be.**'
>
> **Michele Tinazzo, car designer**

you should create at least two 2D views of the product. This is done by creating a secondary view that relates to the original's details, as seen in **fig. 7.8**. Select all the visual features that will be seen in the new view, and sketch faint straight lines (pink in our illustration) from those features to another centre line, to ensure they are correctly aligned. Experienced designers can sketch new designs in three dimensions quickly without these views, but 2D views are essential for ensuring the mechanical or electrical components can be packaged.

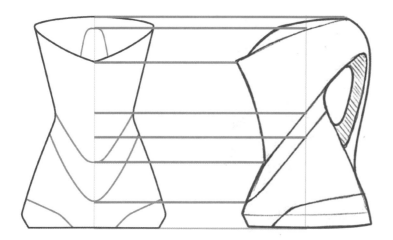

7.8 Creating a front view from a side view: orthographic projection

Chapter overview

Define the volumes that appear to be undesirably bulky, boxy or large, and experiment by sketching over them with the following options:

01 | **Adjust the size or position of visual features to fill the volume better.**

02 | **Try cloning a large volume's silhouette inwards to create a smaller volume inside. Could this volume become a new component, a cavity or a contrasting indentation?**

03 | **Experiment by sketching lines or shapes that could become surface changes that will separate the volume.**

04 | **If the product will be shiny, surface reflections can help to separate volumes (see Chapter 8).**

05 | **Try adding colours or graphics to improve the division of volumes.**

Case study: Electric Kettle

The water-level indicator in the sketch at the top runs across the main body of the kettle at an angle, from the handle down to the front of the product. This feature also has a stylistic function: to add visual interest and split up the main volume of the kettle, reducing its visual bulk. The second design, without this division, looks cleaner, but also heavier because of the apparently larger main volume. The irregular silhouette of this volume adds impact and reduces boxiness.

You can now decide whether to develop the 2D concept into three dimensions by continuing through the book, or to focus on a range of other 2D styling options.

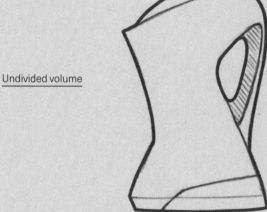

Divided volume

How volume division affects visual weight.

Undivided volume

Chapter 8

Surface

Learning objectives

- Define the term 'surface' in relation to a product (page 102).

- Identify the three types of surface: convex, concave and planar (page 104).

- Explain the visual effect of increasing or decreasing surface angles (page 106).

- Demonstrate an understanding of how reflective surfaces mirror their environment (page 107).

- Discuss the effects of surface detail (page 107).

- Describe five commonly used surface methods: smooth transitions, tension, double curvature, definition, chamfering (pages 108–111).

- List the four main types of surface continuity (page 112).

- Experiment with surface design using contour lines or shading (page 113).

- Summarize the ways in which surface design can improve a product (page 114).

Chapter 8
Surface

Surfaces fill the gaps between sketched lines. They are the meat on the bones of any product, and as a designer, you must think like a sculptor as you enter three dimensions. Surfaces can be very emotive when styled in conjunction with thoughtful line design, and they are the main elements that truly arouse a consumer's visual passion for a product (**fig. 8.1**). Depending on the design brief, it is possible to manipulate a product's surface language to evoke anything from muscular power to gentle purity.

Designers use surfaces to manipulate light and shadow for visual effect and to unite the 3D form. Surfaces can optimize the form of a product when functional constraints abound. By incorporating illusions such as 'light-catchers' (upward-facing areas that appear brighter than neighbouring surfaces), designers can move closer to an ideal form. Surfaces can enhance character, and can help a product to look lighter by separating or softening volumes with light and shadow. Athletic

8.1 Ferrari SF90 Stradale, 2019, muscular surface design and light-catching surfaces

'When I was young, all we ever heard about was functionalism, functionalism, functionalism. It's not enough. Design should also be sensual and exciting.'

Ettore Sottsass, architect and designer

8.2 Athletic shoes have complex undulating surfaces that mimic the human foot

shoes have some of the most complex surface designs of any product, because they have to wrap around the complex form of the human foot. In the example illustrated in **fig. 8.2**, additional surface details add character. The bicycle helmet in **fig. 8.3** has complex surfaces that twist and flow beneath one another and around the form. Echoed shape highlights in the surfaces exploit light and shadow to divide the dynamic form, and contrasting material finishes increase visual separation. This kind of dynamic surface design never fails to grab the consumer's attention, but much simpler surfacing can also be desirable, depending on the target market.

8.3 Giro Ember MIPS women's bicycle helmet, 2018

The simple geometric surfaces of the watch in **fig. 8.4** provide an air of precision and robustness – important criteria for certain products. The edges have been chamfered to catch the light as the wrist moves. These little details, which are often polished to maximize their reflectivity, accentuate the precision of the timepiece. This particular design is also nostalgic, since it resembles classic aircraft cockpit instrumentation.

8.4 Bell & Ross BR 03-92 wristwatch, 2018

Light and shadow

When a shiny surface is angled towards the ground, it will reflect the ground colour (or shadow). If the surface is angled upwards, it will look lighter in daylight or artificial light. As we have seen, most 'lines' apparent on products are shut lines (which are in shadow), component edges or surface creases that are highlighted when light hits them. So, when it comes to the 3D modelling stage, your sketched lines will become shut lines, edges, surface creases or component shapes (solid or empty). When styling, it is good practice to imagine what each line might become, to understand the 3D form better.

Surface types and angles

Three types of surface are available to the designer – convex, concave and planar (**fig. 8.5** shows these surfaces in section) – as well as any combination of the three.

8.5 Convex surfaces (top) project outwards; concave surfaces (centre) 'cave' inwards; and planar surfaces (bottom) are flat

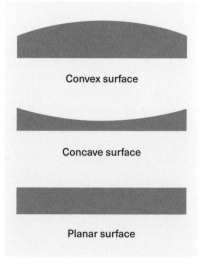

Convex surface

Concave surface

Planar surface

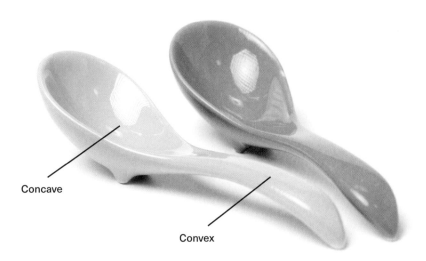

Concave

Convex

Surfaces can be a hybrid of concave and convex, as illustrated in **fig. 8.6**. This demonstrates how surface experimentation and innovation can result in a new visual that grabs the viewer's attention.

Surfaces can be designed on paper using contour lines or by rendering, but it is only when 3D modelling begins (physical or digital) that a designer can resolve the surfaces of a complex product accurately. Sculptural surfaces must always be viewed from various angles to ensure they blend across neighbouring features and surfaces. Convex surfaces can look over-inflated if they are not styled with care. The beautifully sculpted convex wheel arch seen in **fig. 8.7** is voluptuous and sensual, without appearing over-inflated.

Chapter Eight | Surface

8.7 Ferrari 250 Testa Rossa Spyder, 1958

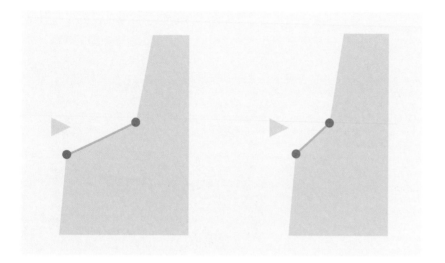

8.8 Deeper surface = more contrast. Shallower surface = less contrast

The deeper and more angled a surface is carved into a product, the bolder it will appear. Imagine chopping a product in half and peering down the open end of one of its surfaces. **Fig. 8.8** shows a cross-section through a product's surfaces, with the pink dots depicting the severed crease lines. If the horizontal distance between the pink dots is greater (assuming the height cannot change), the green surface becomes more inclined and therefore reflects more light. This will give more contrast than with the steeper grey surfaces when seen from the side (grey arrows). If the distance between the pink dots is shortened, the surface angle becomes steeper, reflecting less light and appearing less contrasted than the previous surface.

This method of staggering neighbouring surface angles to adjust the contrast of reflected light is especially useful when you are attempting to reduce the visual bulk of larger volumes (**fig. 8.9**; see also Chapter 7).

8.9 Bosch PST 18 LI cordless jigsaw, 2016, with staggered surface contours highlighted in blue

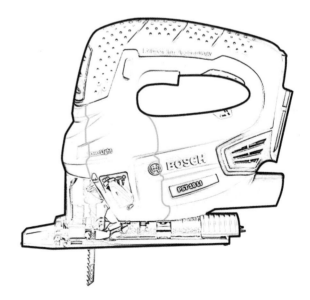

Reflective surfaces

Reflective surfaces are naturally broken up by mirroring their surroundings. Look at how the shiny sphere and body of the lamp in **fig. 8.10** achieve this. Bare surfaces may not need embellishment if they are reflective, because the reflections that play on them may provide enough visual interest and separation.

It is important to understand how reflective surfaces mirror their environment, as this will enable you to control the resulting reflections and gradients that appear on your surfaces. The best way to learn is to observe simple reflective geometry, such as that of a cylinder, a sphere, a cube or a cone. If a design has complex surfacing that will be reflective or shiny, it is a good idea to model it in CAD, and produce a rendering. You can then check and optimize the surface design until the reflections work with the design of the product.

8.10 A shiny surface will reflect its environment

Surfaces in detail

The mouse in **fig. 8.11** has been split visually into two main volumes. The surfaces above the side buttons appear brighter than those below, helping to reduce its visual mass. All the surfaces above the side buttons are angled upwards, and most below it are angled down. The brighter surface at the bottom may have been designed to provide some support to the thumb, or simply to catch the viewer's eye.

8.11 TeckNet M003 mouse

Surfaces can also be designed to suggest methods of use. The sander (**fig. 8.12**) has a rounded form with elliptical indentations in the side surfaces for the user's thumb and fingers to grasp either side while sanding.

The helmet shown in **fig. 8.13** has surface details known as light-catchers that add highlights, increasing visual interest and dynamism without the need for extra graphics or cavities that could reduce the helmet's crash-worthiness. The light-catchers consist of crisp highlight 'lines' formed where two opposing surfaces meet, with enough depth to provide good definition. These are the lines that the designer would have sketched in side profile. The surfaces above the lines merge gradually into the side in a concave manner to catch the light, while the dark surfaces below are angled to face the ground. Light-catchers can also be used to disguise less desirable details by placing them in shadow, or to alter a side profile with an undesirable silhouette. The helmet appears both less cluttered and less dynamic without the light-catchers; both could be desirable traits, depending on the design brief and the target customer.

8.12 Black & Decker Mouse sander, 2015

Surface methods

Smooth transitions

Attractive surfaces generally have smooth horizontal and vertical transitions between lines. The damaged surface illustrated in **fig. 8.14** is unappealing because of the lack of smoothness in the surfaces and

8.13 Bell MX-9 Adventure helmet, 2015. On the right, with light-catchers removed

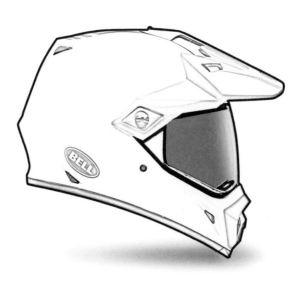

8.14 A damaged surface
producing random light effects

the randomness of light and shadow that results.
Compare the damaged surface with the fluid and
controlled surfaces in **fig. 8.15** that flow with grace
and purpose, forming an immediate emotional
connection with the viewer.

Tension

Surface tension can be used to create the illusion of
pent-up energy or motion. Examine the surface of
the rubber band that is being twisted and stretched
(**fig. 8.16**). The tension is visible on the surface in the
form of gentle tapering and gradient shadows.

8.15 Philips GC5039/30 Azur
Elite Steam Iron, 2018

8.16 Rubber band
under tension

8.17 Bosch EasyPrune cordless secateurs (pruners), 2018

Tension has been incorporated into the lower handle of the secateurs (pruners) shown in **fig. 8.17**, using a combination of tapered lines and gentle surface rotation.

Double curvature

Double curvature is when a surface curves in two directions (or planes). It looks softer and more natural than a geometric single-curvature surface.

The main silver surface of **fig. 8.18** has double curvature, which creates a soft, spherical gradient reflection across it. Note that the designer has also made the base look thin and lightweight by darkening the sides; as a result, the silver surface looks delicate and elegant, as if it were a sheet of silk. Compare this surface with the silver surface of **fig. 8.19**, which looks much heavier purely because of its perceived thickness.

> **Double curvature looks softer and more natural than a geometric single-curvature surface.**

8.18 Philips HR2094 blender, 2002

Definition

Bold, well-defined surfaces provide visual complexity and give an impression of good quality. Deep surfaces that cut into the product create more contrast between light and shadow, producing a more pronounced, confident effect. Alternating convex and concave surfaces joined by tight radii result in crisp surface crease lines, as in fig. 8.19. Larger radii will blend the surfaces, reducing line definition; this is typically found in products with a softer form language.

Chamfering

Chamfered edges create an air of precision, and are often used to achieve neat edge highlights, as seen in **fig. 8.20**. A chamfer is technically a planar surface at a 45-degree angle to the mating surfaces, but in product styling it can be described in a much broader sense. The coffee machine in fig. 8.19, for example, has a chamfered surface running along the top right-hand edge of the silver panel that sweeps down towards the front. However, this chamfer is not 45 degrees and is softened by being slightly curved, demonstrating the flexibility of this type of surface.

8.19 Philips Saeco coffee machine, 2010

Chapter Eight | Surface

8.20 JiGMO voice recorder, 2017

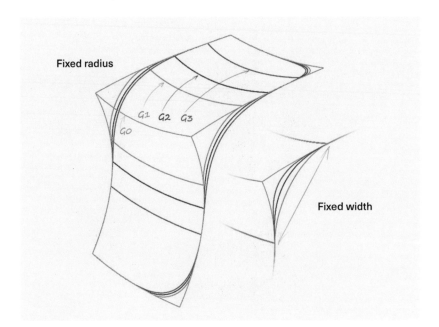

Surface continuity

There are four main types of surface continuity that are useful to understand at the CAD modelling stage (**fig. 8.21**). G0 are connected surfaces without continuity, creating a highlighted edge when catching the light. G1 continuity is a surface that is tangential to the opposing surfaces, and creates a controlled highlight near the radius. G2 continuity also indicates a tangent, but an extended one, which means that the reflections will be much smoother throughout. Finally, G3 continuity creates a seamless join between surfaces, as found typically in automotive design.

Modelling clay and Styrofoam are materials that designers commonly use to perfect surfaces at the modelling stage. It is important to have a good idea of the types of surface you require on paper before you spend time modelling in a workshop. Complete all the necessary package drawings so that you can understand better how deep the surfaces can cut into the product without affecting the internal components. Some products will have additional requirements controlled by regulatory bodies such as BSI (British Standards Institution) in the United Kingdom, UL (Underwriters Laboratories) in the United States and IEC (International Electrotechnical Commission) in Europe, so it is important to understand and conform to those where necessary. Once this has been established, you can create a model with confidence, knowing the surfaces will not compromise the package.

Surface design

Once you have completed a sketch of your product, there are several ways to experiment with surface design. Designers often sketch contour lines on to their concepts to show the design intent (the pink lines in **fig. 8.22**). Shading and colour rendering are the clearest ways of adding surface form, but they take more time. In the end, the client will always have more faith in a rendered image or a physical model than in a simple sketch.

Surface transitions are most likely to occur where there are lines or shapes, so if you are unsure about where a surface change might occur, it's a good idea to start experimenting in those areas. Adobe Photoshop is a useful rendering tool to add form, because you can save time by making alterations without having to produce many sketches. It is wise to have to hand a 2D image of a competing product that you can use as a guide. The surfaces should blend with the overall product form language influenced by the original visual theme.

The shaver in **fig. 8.23** has an organic, hi-tech feel with its soft, defined surfaces. This is the perfect surface language for this product, since

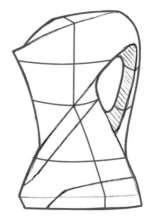

8.22 Contour lines (top) and rendering clarify the form

8.23 Braun Series 7 Electric Shaver, 2016

it is designed to fit the hand. If a product is to be handled regularly by
the user, it is crucial to design sympathetic ergonomic surfaces or it
will not appear or feel comfortable to hold. Experimentation is essential
to achieve attractive surfaces that will meet ergonomic requirements,
gel with the rest of the product and reflect its environment in the most
appealing manner.

Chapter overview

There are three types of surface available to designers:
convex, concave and planar. Try incorporating some of
these by contouring, shading or rendering the 2D views
to see what would be most appropriate. Experiment with
tension, double curvature, definition, chamfers and radii,
while maintaining smooth transitions across the product.
While sketching, try to visualize how different surfaces might
work with your design. Surfaces can improve a product in
the following ways:

01 | **They can lighten a product visually by separating or softening volumes with light and shade.**

02 | **Surface highlights and reflections add visual interest, as well as reducing the apparent size of large volumes.**

03 | **The more deeply and more angled a surface carves into a product, the bolder it will appear.**

04 | **Light surfaces draw the viewer's eye towards more attractive areas, and less desirable volumes can be disguised by placing them in shadow.**

05 | **Ensure your surfaces are fit for function. For example, if the product is to be used or kept outdoors, ensure that its concave surfaces will not collect rainwater (unless they are intended to do so). Softer surfaces with large radii may be necessary if the product is to be handled for long periods.**

Case study: Electric Kettle

The rendering of the kettle here suggests that its form is a slightly stretched cylinder at the top (silver) and conical at the bottom (dark grey). The silver surface has tension as it sweeps from spout to handle, adding visual impact. The more geometric conical surface at the bottom provides a solid footprint for the kettle, while ensuring that it holds enough water.

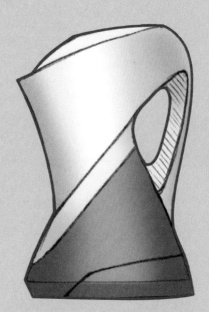

Rendered 2D kettle surface language.

Once the surfaces have been completed in two dimensions, you should feel confident with your 2D views. If the design still has visual flaws, try to understand the problem areas and innovate to provide options that will resolve them. It is a good idea to take a break from the design or work on another view at this stage, to refresh your eyes; you will find that you spot and fix visual flaws more easily on your return. The next stage is to make your design work in three dimensions.

Chapter 9

2D to 3D

Learning objectives

- Identify the most common methods of 3D sketching (page 118).

- Describe how to use an existing design guide to aid 3D styling (page 119).

- Explain how to check proportions when translating from two to three dimensions (page 120).

- Outline the ways in which visual proportions can be changed without altering overall size (page 120).

- Explain the need for adjusting lines when moving into three dimensions (page 123).

- Analyse successful examples of 3D styling (page 123).

- Summarize the main points of converting two to three dimensions (page 126).

Chapter 9
2D to 3D

Transforming your 2D designs into three dimensions essentially involves joining them together. Products are objects that will be seen from many angles, so it is important that the 2D views work together when merged into 3D form. The skill in 3D styling is getting the perspective correct and being able to merge the relevant 2D views in a natural, seamless manner that reflects the original design intent. A common method of learning 3D sketching is to draw a box in one- or two-point perspective with the desired proportions, and fill the relevant faces with the foreshortened 2D views, blending them at the intersections. This can take years to master, however, and becomes frustrating when all you want is to produce a representative 3D image of a concept, quickly.

Sketching in perspective must be studied and practised, but 3D design guides (which are also used by professionals) will help you to produce accurate results in less time. By using a 3D design guide as an underlay and sketching an original design over it, you will also begin to understand the nuances of 3D form and perspective.

Sketching in three dimensions is difficult, but it is useful to be able to judge, present and alter the styling of a 3D product quickly. Three-dimensional sketching allows you to control the design precisely, and allows clients or managers to understand your vision easily. There are many books and digital tutorials, but dedicated daily practice with design guides will enable you to improve quickly. If sketching is not your thing, you could make physical or digital models instead, but they tend to take more time.

Move into physical or digital modelling as soon as a concept has been selected to better understand and perfect the form.

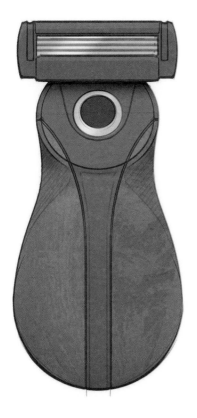

Three-dimensional styling should begin with a 3D view that will be most commonly seen by the user, for example a rear three-quarter view, as seen in **fig. 9.1** (right). Find a suitable 3D design guide for an existing product with similar proportions to use as an underlay. (These images can easily be found online.) Trace it on to layout paper, adding the perspective guidelines and vanishing points, then repeat the process, adjusting the position and styling of some visual features. When you feel confident, try to recreate your own design in this view while referring to the 2D views you have already created. With time and practice the design guides can be removed, and when you feel confident, you can begin styling in three dimensions without guides.

For a product to look appealing in three dimensions, several guidelines should be followed. First, you should transfer the completed 2D designs accurately into a 3D sketch or model. If 3D sketching is still a developing skill for you, it may take you several attempts to get it right. Once you are happy that your sketch does the 2D views justice, you can move on to the next step. Designers often use artistic licence in the early stages of 3D sketching to improve the visual flow across a product, which is why it is important to move into physical or digital modelling as soon as a concept has been selected, so that you can better understand and perfect the form.

9.1 Three-dimensional concept razor sketch by Tom McDowell, 2018

3D proportions

When stylistically critiquing a 3D sketch, your first step should be to ensure that the overall proportions appear as originally proposed in two dimensions. Check the relation of width, length and height, and tweak the proportions if the package and functional constraints allow. The spacing and proportions of the visual features should also be checked and modified if required, since they may look different in three dimensions owing to the effect of foreshortening – an optical illusion whereby elements appear smaller as their distance from the viewer increases. Photoshop is a useful tool for experimenting with the proportions of a sketch, as they can be tweaked quickly using the 'transform' tool. Examples of proportional adjustment can be seen in **fig. 9.2**.

Proportional illusions

If your design needs proportional adjustment overall but the extremities cannot be altered, it may be possible to lengthen or shorten its apparent proportions by adjusting the visual features. Longer features make a product look longer, and shorter features do the opposite. This can trick the viewer into visualizing a longer or shorter overall volume that is closer to the designer's intention, when in reality it has not changed.

The images in **fig. 9.3** show the difference between wider and narrower heater grilles. The first design looks slightly longer than the second, but the heaters are both the same length.

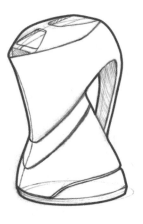

9.2 Kettle with differing overall proportions (height unchanged)

9.3 Dimplex Essentials convector heater, 2008. Right, with a smaller grille that makes the product appear narrower

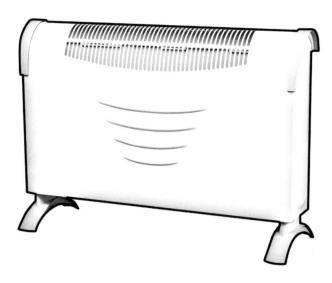

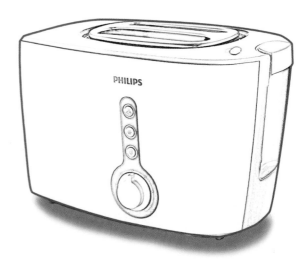

You can adjust a product's apparent proportions in three dimensions by increasing or decreasing the curvature at the corners. By reducing curvature at one end, as illustrated in **fig. 9.4**, you can make a product look longer.

9.4 Philips HD2636/20 toaster, 2018. Right, with the left-hand corner radii reduced to make the product look longer

Reducing boxiness

When a design looks undesirably boxy in three dimensions, it may be possible to disguise that fact by modifying its plan view (**fig. 9.5**, left). By adding generous radii to the corners (pink lines) and slight side curvature (green line), as seen in the view below right, the designer can blend the corners and side panels, creating a more rounded form when seen in three dimensions.

9.5 Apple Magic mouse, 2008. Right, with corner radii and side curvature highlighted

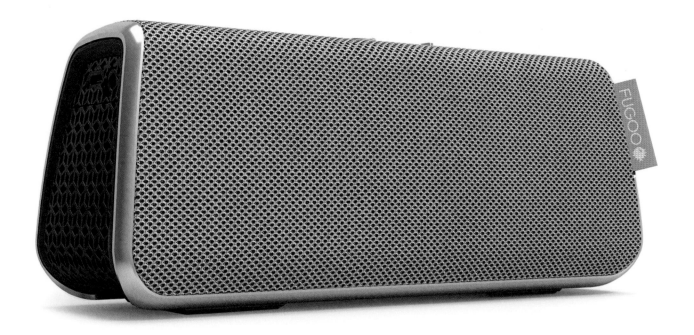

Boxiness can be disguised by removing one of the sides. The speaker in **fig. 9.6** is essentially a cuboid, but the designer has disguised its sides, reducing its otherwise boxy, 3D appearance.

Another way to reduce boxiness is to soften the shapes of the visual features, as seen in **fig. 9.7**. A microwave oven must have a planar rectangular silhouette if it is to fit neatly into a compact kitchen environment, but the rounded features soften the overall appearance.

9.6 Fugoo Style bluetooth speaker, 2014

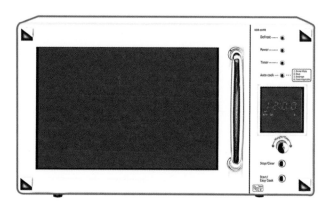

9.7 Daewoo KOR6N9RW microwave, 2012. The design of visual features affects the appearance of the entire product. Right, the boxy appearance is enhanced

3D lines

Once you have perfected the proportions, you can focus on making sure the lines and shapes still look right in three dimensions. Some lines may not flow across a 3D form as well as you intended, owing to the concave or convex surfaces they must traverse, so you may need to alter their paths to perfect continuity in the chosen view. Visual relationships to neighbouring lines or visual features may also need minor adjustments. When moving into three dimensions, focus on retaining 2D line curvature, if applicable, to retain the character of the original design. In the following examples we discuss what you should be looking for during 3D styling.

3D styling analysis

Savora peeler

This humble peeler (**fig. 9.8**) has quite a complex form. A teardrop shape is the main theme, as highlighted by the chromed handle. This volume is mirrored to the front, where a concave surface cradles the cutting blade. This rounded concave form flows to the rear in an elegant 'S' curve when viewed in side profile (see page 42). The form works well in three dimensions, and the silhouette is smooth and therefore easy on the eye.

9.8 Savora Swivel Blade peeler, 2013

'The details are not the details. They make the design.'

Charles Eames, product designer

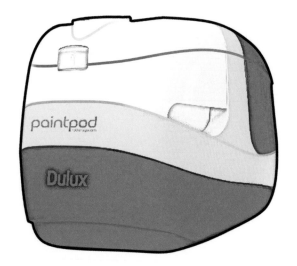

9.9 Dulux PaintPod, 2010

Dulux PaintPod

The product styling (**fig. 9.9**) is simple yet elegant in three dimensions. The lines flow in soft, wave-like fashion across its surfaces (pink and orange lines), and although it is essentially a box, it does not look boxy. The corners have been softened with large radii and the sides have double curvature, which improves 3D line continuity from front to side. The lines and colours divide the main volume into sections, and the functional grey frame adds to the robust and distinctive appearance. The grey frame and blue base resemble a classic wicker basket, which may be connected to a styling theme of eco-friendliness and simplicity.

Opel Meriva concept car

There is a graceful yet purposeful system of lines across the surfaces of the car in **fig. 9.10**. As with many vehicles, most lines begin their journey at the branded front grille, forming the bonnet shut line and

9.10 Opel Meriva concept car, 2008. On the right, with lines blending with complex surfaces creating a coherent 3D visual

sweeping up into the A pillar and across the roof (pink line). The bonnet shut line could have taken a wider path by merging with the side of the headlight, but the designer chose the more graceful path from grille to A pillar. The inside edge of the headlight (blue line) is almost parallel with the neighbouring bonnet line, which adds relation, and then gently tapers away from it, adding dynamism. The lower grille has a surface crease (green line) that curves up towards the outside edge of the headlight, and is also parallel to the side of the front grille and headlight (pink and blue). The fog-light recess (orange) by the front wheel relates to the lower grille surface crease (green line) and wheel arch, and its shape resembles that of the headlight, for visual consistency. The flank surface detail (turquoise line) relates to the top of the front wheel arch, although there is space between them. The design team was unable to make all the lines flow perfectly across this vehicle. The surface crease line that extends from the end of the headlight towards the side window (red circle) appears slightly awkward, because it is so close to being in-line with the belt line below it.

Philips dry iron

The iron in **fig. 9.11** has a clean, organic appearance, which is refreshing when compared with the typically fussy, hi-tech-looking products on the market. The first feature that draws the eye is the blue section that runs elegantly up from the front and across the handle. In fact, all the important interaction points are blue (handle, resting plate and control knob), which helps the user while also adding visual interest. There is a faint linear pattern in the handle that is echoed near the base of the product. This is reminiscent of a whale's ventral grooves, which may be intended to evoke eco-friendliness or grace and therefore efficiency. The product's main styling feature is the eye-shaped handle cavity that is cloned inwards from the silhouette when seen from the side. This creates a pleasing soft volume in three dimensions that breaks up and lightens the overall design.

9.11 Philips GC160 dry iron, 2013

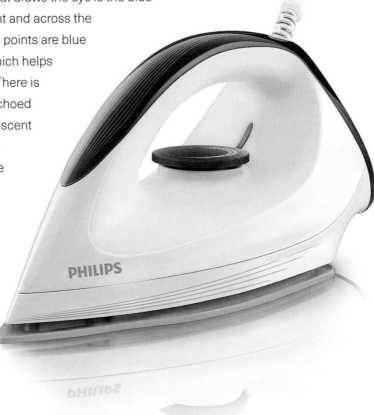

Once the 3D views are complete, you can begin to sculpt a 3D physical
or digital model to refine the form. As the form evolves, cast your
eye across each surface from different viewpoints, to ensure they
flow smoothly across the product from all angles. It is a good idea to
take photographs of physical models in progress, print them out and
highlight areas that could be improved. You can then sketch over the
images to suggest alternative options.

Once the surfaces have been modelled in CAD or physically, the
surface reflections and highlights can be critiqued. You should
essentially be aiming for smooth reflections and controlled transitions
of light and shadow across the product. Jerky or unappealing highlights
that suddenly jump across surfaces should be improved if possible.

Chapter overview

Sketch a 3D view of the product by bonding the relevant
2D views in a natural, seamless manner. Use a 3D product
guide that has similar proportions to the proposed design
to create an accurate sketch, and be aware of the following:

01 | **Check the overall 3D relation of width, length and height, and tweak the proportions if required and if it is functionally viable.**

02 | **The spacing and proportion of the visual features should also be critiqued and modified if necessary, since they may look slightly different in three dimensions.**

03 | **Check that all lines relate to neighbouring lines, visual features or shapes, so that they have logical starting and end points. Well-related design elements help to unite the 3D form.**

04 | **Could some elements be altered in three dimensions to create a more graceful path across the product in the chosen three-quarter view?**

05 | **Do all the surfaces intersect in the most appealing way possible?**

06 | **If you are creating a physical 3D model, take photographs of it, print them out and highlight areas that could be improved. Try to enhance the design by sketching alternative lines over these areas.**

Case study:
Electric Kettle

At this stage, your aim is to visualize the product in three dimensions, often using artistic licence to achieve the best result, because the form has not yet been completely defined. Once you have sketched the basic form, you may need to fine-tune it to improve line flow and relation across the product.

The 3D view (above right) was selected to expose the design of the lid. It is a translation of the 2D views created earlier (see page 99), with modifications to improve the continuity of the lines. The water-level detail sweeps around the front of the kettle and merges into the top of the handle. The lid was designed to incorporate a finger hole for opening. The main user interaction points, highlighted in blue in the sketch below right – lid, water-level indicator and handle – provide a hi-tech feel.

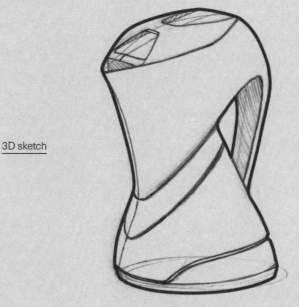

3D sketch

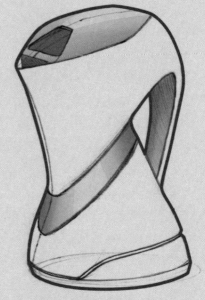

Detail rendering

Chapter 10

Colour

Learning objectives

- Demonstrate the importance of colour in relation to trends and emotional response (page 130).

- Explain the use of contrast in colour styling (page 132).

- Summarize the main considerations when selecting colours (page 134).

Chapter 10
Colour

Colour is a vast subject in product design, and greatly influences the appearance and desirability of consumer products, as well as increasing brand recognition. This chapter provides a brief introduction to colour, focusing on how you can use it to enhance the design and styling of your products. Colours go in and out of fashion and have different meanings to different cultures, so it is essential to keep track of current and predicted colour trends (www.pantone.com is a useful resource for all the latest fashion colour trends). A product can look outdated or undesirable if it is an unfashionable or unsuitable colour, and, as a designer, you must ensure that the colours you choose meet the target customer's expectations and suit the image of the brand.

Colour and user response

Colours are linked to our emotions, a fact that enables designers to enhance desirable feelings and moods by stimulating or calming the user visually. Red attracts attention, for example, which is why it is

10.1 Bosch Uneo drill, 2017, with red controls that aid first-time usability

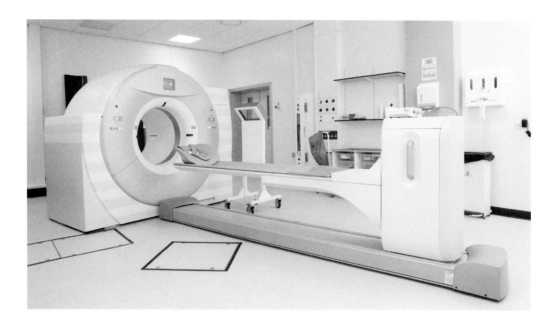

commonly used to highlight emergency controls or important user interactions, as seen in **fig. 10.1**. By using the same red for all user interactions, the ease of first-time use is improved as the points of contact become clearer.

When selecting colours for medical products, the patient's mental condition and environment should be considered. For instance, calming pastel colours are more suitable than intense colours for use in hospitals (**fig. 10.2**). It is common for toothbrushes to be white, because of that colour's association with cleanliness and perhaps also owing to our desire for white teeth. A dark yellow toothbrush (**fig. 10.3**) would no doubt sell very poorly, however stylish the design. Many kitchen appliances are also white, because this neutral colour tends to blend in to the environment without stealing the limelight.

10.2 Siemens Biograph CT hospital scanner, introduced in 2008, with calming pastel colour

Chapter Ten Colour

10.3 Dark yellow may not be the best choice for a toothbrush

'Having small touches of colour makes it more colourful than having the whole thing in colour.'

Dieter Rams, product designer

Traditionally, blue has been considered masculine and pink feminine, especially when it comes to children's products. But it would be a mistake simply to add one of these colours to a product and expect it to appeal to the target audience. If a product is to be aimed at a specific gender, the design itself should appeal to the customer before colour is added.

Styling contrast

The most useful aspect of colour for product styling is contrast. A product's components have to be a certain size to function correctly but if they are too large they can become disproportionate to the rest of the product and will not look right. Designers get around this problem by splitting the main body into multiple volumes and making them darker. The product at **fig. 10.4** uses vibrant coloured volumes and darker, matt volumes. The darker areas are less apparent, as the eye is drawn to the more vibrant section (which should also be the more attractive area). This method may not work if the main colour of the product is black or another dark shade, because the contrast will be reduced.

10.4 Philips SpeedPro Max Cordless Stick Vacuum Cleaner 8000, 2018

Designers sometimes use metallic colours or materials to highlight important features. It is common to see chrome strips surrounding control panels, displays or front grilles, for example. The use of chrome in design reached its peak in the 1950s; it is used more discreetly nowadays. Colours, materials or textures that draw the eye are useful for highlighting functionally important or aesthetically meaningful areas of a product.

Darker tones, on the other hand, can be used to make visually undesirable features less prominent. It is common to see dark window pillars on cars, to reduce the visual disruption they create. This makes the side window appear as a single integrated shape, rather than several smaller volumes that disrupt the horizontal dynamic shape, as seen in **fig. 10.5**.

10.5 Land Rover Evoque coupé glasshouse, 2014, top. Below, with lighter pillars for comparison

In summary, the most useful aspect of colour for product styling is contrast, as it helps to break up larger volumes and highlight the visually appealing areas. Colours are linked to our emotions, so understand the target customer's preferences before selecting shades. Colours can also be used to highlight emergency controls and important user interactions.

Chapter overview

If a product or component appears undesirably bulky or the overall silhouette is unappealing because of functional restrictions, it is possible to disguise its form in the following ways:

01 | Divide the product proportionally (see Chapter 3) and add a primary colour to one half, leaving the rest dark grey. The more vibrantly coloured volume will stand out against the dark half, making it more noticeable and therefore disguising the bulk and silhouette of the product as a whole.

02 | When selecting colours for a product, it is best to choose one principal colour and add splashes of metallic finishes (chrome or aluminium) or a contrasting colour to highlight interaction points.

03 | Also consider the following:

(A) Whether the chosen colour's association is appropriate for the target audience.

(B) The user's possible psychological condition.

(C) The environment in which the product may be used.

(D) Whether the product is suitable for different cultures (if it is to be sold worldwide).

(E) The colours suggested by the mood board.

Case study: Electric Kettle

The upper half of the kettle is to have a brushed-aluminium effect that will draw the eye to the more dynamic half of the product. The base is a dark grey soft-touch polymer that contrasts with the upper half, splitting the design in two visually and making it look lighter.

The aquamarine is translucent, so that the user can see the water level, and so that the water inside looks more refreshing. The user's main points of interaction are in blue to highlight the main interaction points and improve first-time use.

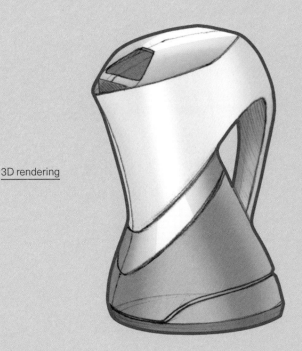

3D rendering

Chapter 11

Materials and texture

Learning objectives

- Explain why certain materials are selected for certain products (page 138).

- Discuss the importance of surface finish and innovative use of materials (page 139).

- Summarize the main considerations when selecting materials (page 140).

Chapter 11

Materials and texture

When it comes to product design, materials are often chosen for their structural integrity, but they can also project visual and tactile information to the customer, who then makes associations and judgements about the product. Customers who have some knowledge of materials may be able to distinguish aluminium from steel, for example, and will realize that the former has the prestige of being used to manufacture aircraft because of its lighter weight and resistance to corrosion. Such associations make a product more desirable to some customers.

> 'I have always appreciated those who dare to experiment with materials and proportions.'
>
> **Zaha Hadid, architect**

Materials and perception

Material selection can affect the look of a product. Some materials have a distinctive pattern that adds character, some are more tactile, and others are simply rare or difficult to extract, which affects cost and desirability. Advanced materials – such as carbon fibre, which gained visibility in high-performance sports such as rowing and Formula One – eventually become the next desirable material for all kinds of product. Materials and finishes, like colours, have a certain lifespan, and designers must ensure that the material itself, or the finish, is on trend for the product category.

Materials say a lot about a product's values. If the goal is for a product to appear environmentally friendly, appropriate natural or recyclable materials should be used. Visually simple products such as the external hard drive in **fig. 11.1** rely heavily on material perception, so the choice of material is critical. This example is made from extruded aluminium, which provides a feeling of quality and durability. Being metal, it is naturally heavier than plastic, and the additional weight adds to the high-quality feel.

11.1 LaCie Porsche Design
P9220 mobile hard drive, 2012

Surface finish

Humans have always been fascinated by shiny objects. Most mobile
phones are visually basic, and most of their desirability comes from
high-quality materials, high-resolution graphics and intuitive user
interaction. However, one of the smartphone's most attractive aspects
is the jewel-like glass display (**fig. 11.2**). This is the part that customers
admire the most, and it is common to see people polishing them to
retain the sparkle even when the phone is not in use.

11.2 Apple iPhone 6, 2014

Innovative material selection can make a product
stand out from the competition.

11.3 Meze 11 Deco wooden earphones, 2013

A fresh, distinctive appearance can be designed by applying materials that are not usually associated with the particular product category. The earphones in **fig. 11.3** have an innovative wooden shell to amplify the warm, eco-friendly appearance, as well as helping them stand out among the competition.

Chapter overview

It is a good idea to ask yourself:

01 | Will the chosen material meet the product's functional requirements (for robustness, temperature resistance, etc.)?

02 | Which materials will the target customer have positive associations with?

03 | Does the chosen material enhance the styling or does it look too busy? Does its tactility enhance the user's experience?

04 | Can a material that is not usually associated with the product category make it stand out?

05 | Which surfaces should the material be applied to? Smothering the whole product in a visually busy material such as carbon fibre may be overpowering for certain demographics.

Case study:
Electric Kettle

Below is a rendering that suggests what the chosen materials might be for our kettle. The exterior is to be made from PP (polypropylene) plastic because it has good heat resistance, is lightweight and cost-effective, and can be translucent. The top half could be electroplated to provide a cost-effective metallic finish, while the lower half could be over-moulded with a soft-touch PU (polyurethane) rubber for a pleasing velvety feel and darker matt finish. The blue components will be translucent blue PP plastic inserts that will allow the user to see the water level.

Chapter 12

Styling projects

Learning objective

- Outline the entire process of styling a series of products from silhouette to materials.

Chapter 12
Styling projects

Below is the entire series of concept sketches demonstrating the styling of a hi-tech kettle. The illustrations should be used as a guide, since not all products will require such comprehensive styling. This kettle did not require any visual volume separation, because the water-level indicator naturally provided adequate surface division. More concept styling examples can be found on pages 149–153.

Example 1: Kettle

<u>Silhouette</u> Below is an example of a new silhouette design. The kettle on the left is a sketch of an existing product that a fictitious client requires restyling into something more hi-tech and distinctive. The designer begins by understanding the design constraints and deciding which areas of the original silhouette could be modified. The spout, handle position and height must match the original product (see the faint outline on the right), but the rest can be manipulated to a certain extent. The new, more distinctive silhouette has already radically changed the appearance of the original, but enough common form remains in the spout and handle for it to be recognizable as a kettle. This silhouette design will evolve throughout the styling process.

For new products, it is preferable to begin styling after the functional elements have been defined. This establishes the constraints you have to work with, as well as the areas where creative freedom can be expressed.

Original design

New silhouette

Proportion The kettle's overall proportions have remained the same as the benchmark kettle. Because it has few major visual features in this 2D view (water-level indicator, lid and base), the designer has instead focused on the silhouette's proportional alignments (below right). It has been designed so that most visual points intersect horizontally or vertically with neighbouring points (pink dots), making the design appear balanced. For example, the tip of the spout is aligned horizontally with the inside arc of the handle, and the water-level indicator is parallel to the lower rear body of the silhouette, all of which creates a more harmonious appearance. With practice you will be able to do this instinctively, without having to add a grid (grey lines). Remember, if a product doesn't look quite right it is usually because of proportional imperfections, so take time to get this stage right.

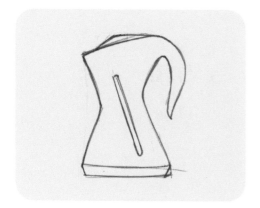

Benchmark design

Alignment points on a grid

Shape The only shape that needed modifying in this case was the water-level indicator, which looked out of place. It was repositioned to be in line with the upper body where it meets the handle, as seen below on the right.

Benchmark design

Water-level indicator repositioned

Stance The first kettle design has a solid, static stance (below left). If a more dynamic stance were desired, the silhouette could simply be tilted, as seen on the right. The weight has been shifted to the front, and the designer has also started to experiment with the styling of the base and handle.

Original design

More dynamic stance

Lines The sketch on the left looks messy, because the designer has been experimenting with line and shape. The water-level indicator is an important visual feature that has been extended across the side of the body, so that it relates to the handle and the silhouette. The designer has also decided to merge the handle back into the body, instead of leaving the end exposed, which creates an empty shape that has been tweaked to intersect with the surrounding lines neatly. Another concept with an unconnected handle could easily be designed as a secondary option. The completed side profile (on the right) has been resketched by overlaying the original to make it more presentable. The silhouette was then darkened to make it stand out.

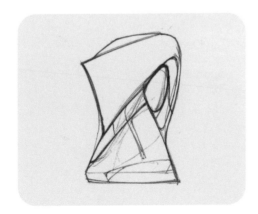

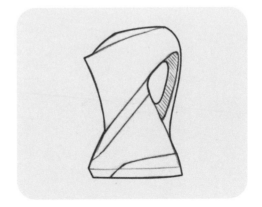

Line experimentation leads to optimized line geometry

Volume The water-level indicator in the sketch below left runs across the main body of the kettle at an angle, from the handle down to the front of the product. This feature also has a stylistic function: to add visual interest and split up the main volume of the kettle, reducing its visual bulk. The second design, without this division, looks cleaner, but also heavier because of the apparently larger main volume. The irregular silhouette of this volume adds impact and reduces boxiness.

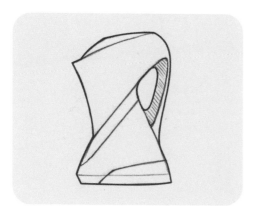 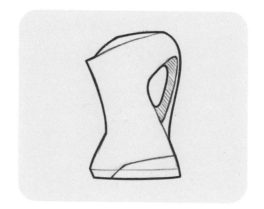

How volume division affects visual weight

Surface The rendering of the kettle below suggests that its form is a slightly stretched cylinder at the top (silver) and conical at the bottom (dark grey). The silver surface has tension as it sweeps from spout to handle, adding visual impact. The more geometric conical surface at the bottom provides a solid footprint for the kettle, while ensuring that it holds enough water.

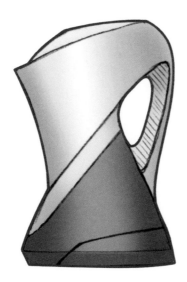

Rendered 2D kettle
surface language

2D to 3D At this stage, your aim is to visualize the product in three dimensions, often using artistic licence to achieve the best result, because the form has not yet been completely defined. Once you have sketched the basic form, you may need to fine-tune it to improve line flow and relation across the product. You may find you need to sketch a 3D view several times before you achieve an accurate depiction, especially with more complex products.

The 3D view below left was selected to expose the design of the lid. It is a translation of the 2D views created earlier, with modifications to improve the continuity of the lines. The water-level detail sweeps around the front of the kettle and merges into the top of the handle. The lid was designed to incorporate a finger hole for opening; this was simplified on the rendered kettle on the right to achieve a cleaner surface detail. The main user interaction points (lid, water-level indicator and handle) are highlighted in blue, and the aluminium upper and dark grey lower volumes provide a hi-tech feel.

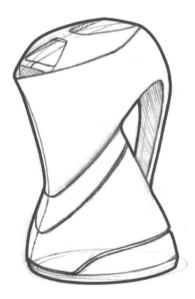
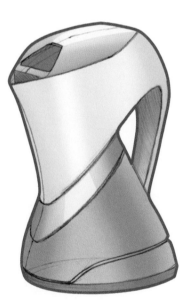

Three-dimensional kettle design
sketch (left) and rendering (right)

Example 2: Motorcycle helmet styling

Robust and aggressive by Mark Detre

The designer has moved away from the traditionally shaped visor here, instead selecting aggressive facial shapes that have influenced the silhouette. The proportions of the 'eyes' have been gradually stretched to improve visibility, and the frown between them has been mirrored to influence the 'nose' vent for a harmonious appearance. The volume of the jaw area has been broken up with a surface crease that has transformed into a concave surface to catch the light.

Benchmark

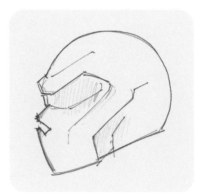

Silhouette

Shape and lines

Stance and volume

3D sketch

Final 3D rendering

Example 3: Hammer

Dynamic and adventurous by Toros Cangar

The head of the hammer was initially simplified and then made more complex when 'adventurous' shapes were incorporated (stalactites and ground contours). Angling the head downwards has given the hammer a dynamic stance, while the handle has become more ergonomic. The empty shape at the neck gives a lighter appearance.

Benchmark

Silhouette

Proportion

Shape and volume

Stance and lines

Surfaces

3D

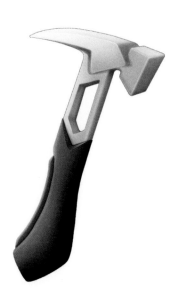

3D rendered

Example 4: Coffee maker styling

Clean and simple by Ian Hadlow

The slightly conical new silhouette creates a more stable, solid stance. The shapes of both the coffee filter and the carafe have been simplified from the benchmark, with added 'running track'-shaped details. Angling the edges of the base has lightened the form, and the concave surface in the carafe clones the handle shape to make room for the user's fingers.

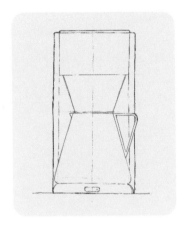

Benchmark

Silhouette

Proportion

Shape and stance

Final 2D

Surfaces

Example 5: Shaver styling

Soft and friendly by Tom McDowell

The designer has taken an ergonomic approach to the razor's silhouette, with a compact, rounded form. The upper circular shape was defined before the lines were ghosted over the form. With the final lines defined, the volumes and surfaces were optimized for comfort. See page 119.

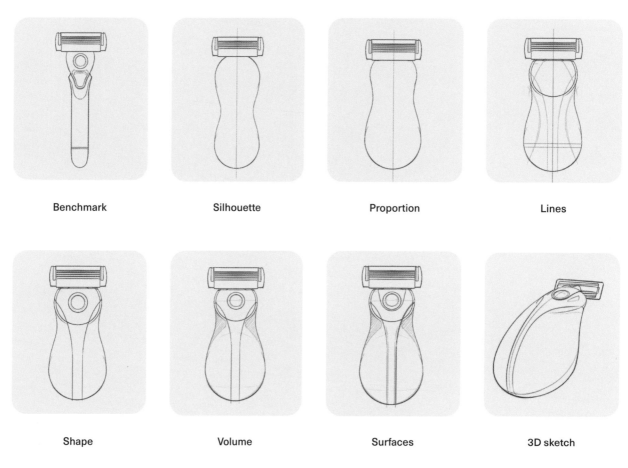

Benchmark	Silhouette	Proportion	Lines

Shape	Volume	Surfaces	3D sketch

3D rendering

Example 6: Athletic shoe

Light and dynamic by Anupam Tomer

The designer had a very clear vision for this shoe and was able to design the silhouette, stance and lines in one pass. The arc at the base of the shoe and the pointed sides make it look lighter. The line around the toe volume has been cloned inwards to create staggered light-catching surfaces at varying angles, while the rear volume, where the foot would be inserted, looks light and dynamic because of its sharp, thin appearance.

Silhouette, stance and lines

Shape and volume definition

Details and branding

Surfaces

Product styling checklist

Glance down this list and decide to use or omit any of the stages that could improve the appearance of your concept. Try to expand on the contents of this book by challenging and innovating as much as possible. Innovative ideas can generate unique styling trends that will make the future of product design more exciting.

☐ **Silhouette**

☐ **Proportion**

☐ **Shape**

☐ **Stance**

☐ **Lines**

☐ **Volume**

☐ **Surface**

☐ **2D to 3D**

☐ **Colour**

☐ **Materials**

Bibliography

Abidin, Shahriman Zainal, Jóhannes Sigurjónsson, André Liem and Martina Keitsch, 'On the Role of Formgiving in Design', *DS 46: Proceedings of E&PDE 2008, the 10th International Conference on Engineering and Product Design Education, Barcelona, Spain, 04–05.09.2008* (2008)

Anderson, Stephen P., *Seductive Interaction Design: Creating Playful, Fun, and Effective User Experiences* (Berkeley, CA: New Riders, 2011)

Baxter, Mike, *Product Design: A Practical Guide to Systematic Methods of New Product Development* (London: Chapman & Hall, 1995)

Bayley, Stephen and Giles Chapman, *Moving Objects: 30 Years of Vehicle Design at the Royal College of Art* (London: Eye-Q, 1999)

Bell, Simon, *Elements of Visual Design in the Landscape* (London and New York: Spon Press, 2004)

Blijlevens, Janneke, Marielle E.H. Creusen and Jan P.L. Schoormans, *How Consumers Perceive Product Appearance: The Identification of Three Product Appearance Attributes* (Delft: Department of Product Innovation Management, Delft University of Technology, 2009)

Bloch, Peter H., 'Seeking the Ideal Form: Product Design and Consumer Response', *Journal of Marketing*, 59:3 (July 1995), p.16

Coates, Del, *Watches Tell More Than Time: Product Design, Information, and the Quest for Elegance* (New York: McGraw-Hill, 2003)

Crilly, Nathan, *Product Aesthetics: Representing Designer Intent and Consumer Response* (Cambridge University Press, 2006)

——, James Moultrie and P. John Clarkson, 'Shaping Things: Intended Consumer Response and the Other Determinants of Product Form', *Design Studies*, 30:3 (May 2009)

Feijs, Loe, Steven Kyffin and Bob Young, 'Design and Semantics of Form and Movement', *DeSForM* (2005)

Useful websites:

www.cardesignnews.com

www.core77.com

www.dezeen.com

www.facebook.com/
PeterStevensDesign

www.getoutlines.com

www.pantone.com

www.yankodesign.com

Bibliography

Hekkert, Paul, 'Design Aesthetics: Principles of Pleasure in Design', *Psychology Science*, 48:2 (2006), pp. 157–72

Kamehkhosh, Parsa, Alireza Ajdari and Yassaman Khodadadeh, *Design Naturally: Dealing with Complexity of Forms in Nature and Applying It in Product Design* (Tehran: College of Fine Arts, University of Tehran, July 2010)

Lenaerts, Bart, *Ever Since I Was a Young Boy I've Been Drawing Cars: Masters of Modern Car Design* (Antwerp: Waft Publishing, 2012)

——, *Ever Since I Was a Young Boy, I've Been Drawing Sports Cars* (Antwerp: Waft Publishing, 2014)

Lewin, Tony and Ryan Borroff, *How to Design Cars Like a Pro* (Minneapolis, MN: Motorbooks, 2010)

Loewy, Raymond, *Never Leave Well Enough Alone* (Baltimore, MD: Johns Hopkins University Press, 1951)

Norman, Donald, *The Design of Everyday Things* (London: MIT Press, 2002)

Powell, Dick, *Presentation Techniques: A Guide to Drawing and Presenting Design Ideas* (Boston, MA: Little, Brown, 1985)

Restrepo-Giraldo, John, *From Function to Context to Form: Supporting the Construction of the Product Image*, International Conference on Engineering Design 05, Melbourne, 15–18 August 2005

Smith, Thomas Gordon, *Vitruvius on Architecture* (New York: Monacelli Press, 2003)

Sparke, Penny, *A Century of Car Design* (London: Octopus, 2002)

References for quotations

p.13, Peter Stevens, 'Aerodynamics: A Technology Tool or a Marketing Opportunity?, Part Two', Facebook post, 21 November 2014, www.facebook.com/PeterStevensDesign/posts/aerodynamics-a-technology-tool-or-a-marketing-opportunity-part-twothe-interestin/875080065858328.

p.19, Stephen P. Anderson, *Seductive Interaction Design*, Chapter 4.

p.31, 'Reborn: The Healey 200', Moss Motoring, 3 August 2015, www.mossmotoring.com/reborn-healey-200.

p.42, Quoted in Roy Ritchie, 'Freeman Thomas, Ford Design Director: Design at the Crossroads of Image and Efficiency', *Automobile* magazine, 3 December 2008, www.automobilemag.com/news/freeman-thomas-ford-design-director.

p.60, Amy Frearson, '"Simplicity Is the Key to Excellence" Says Dieter Rams', Dezeen, 24 February 2017, www.dezeen.com/2017/02/24/dieter-rams-designer-interview-simplicity-key-excellence.

p.82, Del Coates, *Watches Tell More Than Time*.

p.97, Michele Tinazzo in Bart Lenaerts, *Ever Since I Was a Young Boy, I've Been Drawing Sports Cars*, p. 107.

Index

Index

Picture credits

Laurence King Publishing would like to thank and acknowledge below all those companies, brands and individuals who kindly allowed us to publish images of their products.

Back cover photograph: Audi AG.

1 Paul Smith; 2 © Vitra. Photo: Hans Hansen; 8 Brother; 9r Anglepoise; 11a & b Philips; 19 Bang & Olufsen; 21 Groupe Renault; 22 Dyson Technology Ltd; 26 Philips; 27a Philip Ross, www.studiophilipross.nl; 28 Philips; 29a & b Flexi.de; 32 © Alessi; 34 Pure; 37 Canon; 42 Lifetime Brands, Inc; 43b Audi AG; 44 Motorola; 47l Dyson Technology Ltd; 47r Reproduced with Permission of Dell © Dell 2021. All Rights Reserved; 50 Herman Miller; 51 General Motors LLC & 52, used as reference; 51b Mamas & Papas Ltd; 60 TOMY UK; 61a Brother; 62 Gillette Venus; 63a Audemars Piguet; 64 With the permission of Mazda; 65 www.abus.com; 67a URC, www.universalremote.com; 67b Morphy Richards; 68 Bosch Home & Garden; 75a Casa Bugatti; 76 Logitech; 77b Smeg; 78 Paul Smith; 82 Philips; 83 Giro; 84 Remington, Spectrum Brands (UK) Ltd; 85a Philips; 85b © Vitra. Photo: Hans Hansen; 87b, 88–89 BMW Group; 90 Mercury Marine; 94 Etón Corporation; 95bc ARCTIC GmbH; 95br, 96al Reproduced with Permission of Dell © 2021. All Rights Reserved; 96ar Philips; 102 © Ferrari SpA; 103b Giro; 104 © Bell & Ross; 106 Bosch Home & Garden; 107b With the permission of Tecknet Online Ltd; 108a Stanley Black & Decker; 108b Race FX; 109c Philips; 110a Bosch Home & Garden; 110b, 111a Philips; 111b ArcosGlobal.com; 113 Procter & Gamble; 120 © Dimplex; 121a Philips; 122a Fugoo; 123 Lifetime Brands, Inc; 124 Opel-Vauxhall; 125, 132 Philips; 130 Bosch Home & Garden; 133 Land Rover UK (used as reference); 139a With permission from Porsche Design; 140 Meze Audio. Design: Antonio Meze.

Additional credits

9l Fructibus/Wikipedia (CC0); 18l Heritage-Images/National Motor Museum/akg-images; 18r Dan Krauss/Getty Images; 20 Photos: Pexels, Pixabay & Unsplash; 27b Anthony Thomas Gosnay & Antoine Francois Atkinson for Dyson Technology Ltd, A Hand Held Appliance. Patent GB2537511. Published 19th October 2016; 30 *What Laptop* magazine/Future via Getty Images; 33a Artur Rydzewski/Unsplash; 33b Golfxx/Dreamstime.com; 35a GetOutlines.com (CC by 4.0); 35b Dean Bertoncelj/Shutterstock; 43c National Motor Museum/Shutterstock Editorial; 45 Mitrandir/Dreamstime.com; 46 N. D'Anvers, *An Elementary History of Art*, Charles Scribner & Sons, New York, 1895. The Proportions of the Human Figure. https://etc.usf.edu/clipart; 53a Photo: nite_owl/Flickr.com (CC by SA 2.0); 54, 55 Patthana Nirangkul/Shutterstock; 61b Dianut Vieru/Shutterstock; 63b dtopal/Shutterstock; 64 TheOtherKev/Pixabay; 66 Thampapon/Shutterstock; 69 Vudhikul Ocharoen/iStock; 70 Drawing by @hanif_yayan; 74 Dotshock/Dreamstime.com; 75b Sarah Cheriton-Jones/Alamy Stock Photo; 77a Volodymyr Burdiak/Shutterstock; 87a samsonovs/iStock; 95a Peter Dabbs; 95bl Tomislav Pinter/Shutterstock; 96b Drive Images/Alamy Stock Photo; 103a 5 Second Studio/Shutterstock; 105a Jiang Hongyan/Shutterstock; 105b dan74/Shutterstock; 107a Photo: Peter Dabbs; 109a Andrey Eremin/123RF; 109b Yolanda Oltra/Alamy Stock Photo; 112 Image Autodesk, Inc. Used with permission; 119 Drawing: Tom McDowell; 121b Cesare Andrea Ferrari/Shutterstock; 131a Lewis Houghton/Science Photo Library; 131b u_dln5yx2z /Pixabay; 139b scanrail/iStock.